IMAGES
*of England*

# SOUTH
# WILTSHIRE

'THAT'S MY DAD!' GEORGE GODDIN OF NORTH TIDWORTH. Since publishing this image on the front cover of *Salisbury Plain, A Second Selection*, the people and the location have been identified. George Goddin is shown here at the well of the Perrett family house, which stood next to his own WD property in North Tidworth. A WD arrow can be seen on the doors of all five cottages that were situated on the road to Ludgershall, to the right of the Ram Hotel. George married the girl next door, a member of the Crane family. They continued to live there until the houses were condemned at the end of the 1950s. They then moved to a newly built house in Tidworth.

IMAGES
*of England*

# SOUTH
# WILTSHIRE

*Compiled by*
Peter Daniels and Rex Sawyer

TEMPUS

First published 1999
Copyright © Peter Daniels and Rex Sawyer, 1999

Tempus Publishing Limited
The Mill, Brimscombe Port,
Stroud, Gloucestershire, GL5 2QG

ISBN 0 7524 1677 4

Typesetting and origination by
Tempus Publishing Limited
Printed in Great Britain by
Midway Clark Printing, Wiltshire

YE OLDE CHIMES CAFÉ AT AMESBURY IN THE 1930s. Isabella Harbour opened this quaint tea shop in High Street, Amesbury, in the 1930s on the site of Henry Harbour's electical and wireless shop. Mrs Harbour was a lovely lady who is still well remembered in the town. Her tiny café was a popular meeting place for local people, and many tourists were enchanted by its old-world charm. It was a delight to take tea there. The venture continued through the lean years of the Second World War and it eventually closed down in the late 1950s. The premises were then taken over by her daughter, Constance Honaker, who ran a hairdressing salon that has remained as such, with three different proprietors, ever since.

# Contents

Introduction                                           7

1. Salisbury – the Railway Era                         9

2. Around the Nadder Valley                           25

3. Around the Wylye Valley                            51

4. Urchfont to Winterbourne Stoke                     71

5. Amesbury and the Avon Valley                       89

6. Around the Bourne Valley                          111

Acknowledgements                                     128

DRESSED FOR THE OCCASION. Peter Daniels and Rex Sawyer can be seen here with a First World War field gun during a picture shoot at Fort Nelson, Hampshire, in 1996. The Mark II QF quick-firing gun was the most common British artillery piece of its time. From its introduction in 1904, twelve thousand of them were built and together they fired over 100 million rounds. With a range of 6,525 yards and operated by a crew of ten, the gun and limber were pulled by six horses. This particular machine is a rare survivor which is still fully functional. Acquired in 1921 by Sir Charles ffoulkes (then honorary curator and first secretary of the Imperial War Museum) it can now be seen at the Royal Armouries Museum of Artillery at Fort Nelson. The uniforms are preserved by a group of Great War enthusiasts known as the 'Brockhurst Artillery'. (Photograph courtesy of David Perkins)

# Introduction

Edwin Rixon was the foreman of the Chilmark Quarry during the early years of the twentieth century. His day-to-day observations were recorded in large Boots' diaries, and although they are much thumbed and blotched by the ink of those days, they provide fascinating reading. Among details of the eggs laid daily by his hens and the problems of winter floods and rat infestation in his cottage, there are many insights into the problems of stone quarrying below ground. It was these diaries which first fired my desire to find out more about life in the South Wiltshire of that time.

History may be said to be forged by the interaction of the landscape and the people who dwell within it. To many people in the past this meant a fairly routine existence of performing the rural tasks of agricultural activity from seedtime to harvest, and of birth, marriage, and death – cycles that were fulfilled in relative anonymity. But my research often threw up individual men and women of sturdy Wiltshire stock who liked to be different. These characters include men like Rixon the stonemason, who once fought the Chilmark quarry master to obtain long overdue wages owed to the quarrymen (and lost his job in the process!)

So, it is the study of people that brings the greatest fascination, with their infinite capacity for individuality and eccentricity. Today, the ever-intrusive media and the pressures of commercialism seek to impose a 'sameness' to our existence; we find increasing security from the kind of uniformity that modern-day fashion imposes upon us. Perhaps that explains the continuing popularity of books such as this, which reflect, in the main, a simpler and less stressful existence.

Buildings, too, remain to provide insights into the lives of our predecessors. The 'lock-ups', those windowless beehive constructions at Heytesbury and Shrewton, depict rough justice for the village drunk to our more liberal minds (or do they?) The sad ruins of the school, farms and the manor house at Imber tell their own story of simple country life defeated by national expediency. The Flood Houses at Orcheston and Shrewton remind us of more natural disaster across even larger areas of Salisbury Plain. There are rick fires and floods, railway disasters, and army-camp life. It is the interaction of rural people, places and events which we have tried to combine to present early-twentieth century life 'in the raw' before the automobile, the increasing drift of labour to the towns, and two theatres of world war changed country living so radically.

Sadly, bereavement and the scattering of families over wider areas have led to the loss of so much material that would have been useful to the local historian. Remaining pictures like those taken by First World War photographers, often cycling miles across Salisbury Plain to the army camps, are rapidly becoming collectors' items.

Fortunately, in 1956, through the initiative of the Women's Institute, a national competition was held to encourage villagers to create a record of their local communities. Many of these projects are real gems, increasing in social value as the years have passed. Today they remain as loving portraits of the people, places, festivities, superstitions, recipes and other events of rural life now long past. Local historical societies, such as those at Tisbury and the Bourne Valley, have created archive rooms whose contents admirably supplement the County Records Office at Trowbridge and the collections of our county library system.

South Wiltshire, loved by walkers, fishermen and environmentalists alike, has so much to offer but it has to be explored fully to reveal its full potential. Once again, Peter and I have used the river valleys, with their picturesque villages, as the framework for our book. We have allowed ourselves some licence with the boundaries in order that important areas like Mere and East Knoyle, Market Lavington and Urchfont are not overlooked. The lovely chalk valley of the Ebble has had to be left out unfortunately, due to lack of space, but this we hope to rectify next year with a new book featuring Salisbury and its environs.

However, no portrait of South Wiltshire could entirely ignore the central part played by the city of Salisbury. We have decided, therefore, to concentrate on one aspect only – that of the development and importance of the railway system. The romantic era of steam started for Salisbury on 11 June 1856 when the Great Western Railway provided a link between London, Bristol and South Wales. Three years later, a further link with the old Milford Station joined the city centre with the London and South Western Railway, providing a route to Exeter, Plymouth and the far west. Salisbury had become an important junction, and something of its triumphs and disasters are portrayed in this chapter.

Rex Sawyer
Tisbury
July 1999

# One
# Salisbury –
# the Railway Era

*EUGENIE* AT SALISBURY, 1863. Seen here on the platform of this locomotive is Fireman Norwood, who was later to become locomotive foreman at Salisbury. *Eugenie* was the first of a batch of five railway engines designed by Joseph Beattie and built by Heyer, Peacock & Company in 1857. The wheel configuration was '2-2-2' and they were fitted with 78 inch driving wheels. *Eugenie* was some six years old when this photograph was taken.

AN EARLY ENGINE ON THE LONDON & SOUTH WESTERN LINE, 1883. Pictured at Salisbury, this engine, No. 454, was designed by William Adams. Built by Robert Stephenson & Company, a famous railway engineering firm from Newcastle-on-Tyne, it was used on the routes west of Salisbury.

A PARTY OF ENGINE CLEANERS IN SALISBURY, BEFORE 1900. Unfortunately, the names of these individuals have not been recorded but someone has scribbled an address on the back of the original photograph: 4 Grosvenor Terrace, Salisbury. That particular row of dwellings stood in Queens Road and at the time of the picture, Revd Levi Norris and members of his family were living at No. 4. He was associated with the Primitive Methodist Chapel in Fisherton Street. Perhaps one of his daughters was married to a London & South Western Railway employee who is to be seen among those pictured in this group? If you can put names to any of the faces, do let us know.

A PARTY OF ENGINE WORKERS IN SALISBURY, EARLY IN THE TWENTIETH CENTURY. The photograph, taken by Harry Rewse, shows D. Knight, George Mills (engine driver), Henry Collins, Michael Bevan, Morris Penny (with the shovel), 'Fitter' Bird (with the smoke box), ? Offer, ? Rowles, 'Fitter' William Hiscock, and ? Treadgold. The men are pictured in front of a masterpiece of engineering design – a T9 '4-4-0' locomotive. A T9-class steam engine was used on the royal train. Another was employed for the funeral train of Captain Eustace Broke Loraine, who was a victim of the first Royal Flying Corps crash at Larkhill in 1912. His body was transported from Bulford Station to its burial place in Bramford near Ipswich. Pictures of Captain Loraine and details of the accident are to be seen in the two volumes of *Salisbury Plain* from the *Archive Photographs* Series, compiled by the authors of this book.

LONDON & SOUTH WESTERN RAILWAY STAFF AT SALISBURY IN AROUND 1906.
We can see from the style of his headwear that the man standing in the middle of the back row
was, surprisingly, a policeman. At that time, each railway company had its own police force. In
addition to their general police duties, the officers would oversee the crossings and signal boxes
and patrol the line. Many of the old engine drivers, when entering a signal box, continued to
call the signalmen 'Sir', in deference to the days when they were invariably policemen. It is
interesting to note that the 'Porters Bell' lettering and the bell push can still be seen at the front
entrance of Salisbury Station. It was used by cab drivers to summon porters who would escort
the taxi passengers and their bags to their respective trains.

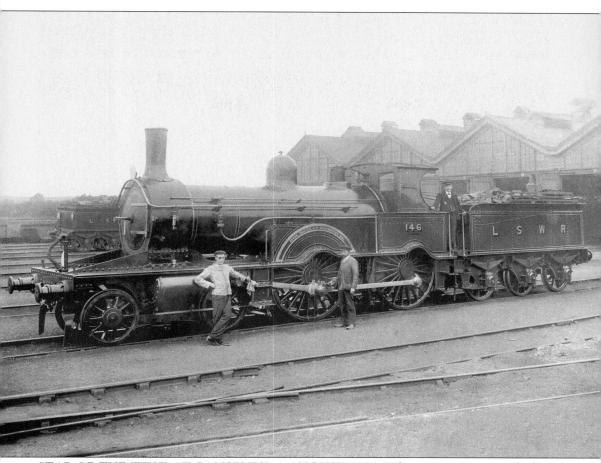

*STAR OF THE WEST* AT SALISBURY, 1 AUGUST 1905. When Harry Rewse took this delightfully nostalgic photograph of locomotive No. 146, it was already twenty-five years old, having been constructed in 1880 by Beyer, Peacock & Company of Manchester. This class of engine was built originally for the Bournemouth and Salisbury lines. An almost identical series of locomotives, but with smaller driving wheels, was built for the lines west of the city. Of the crew pictured here, W. Walsh was the fireman (oil can in hand), A. Hopkins was the driver, and S. Warner was the cleaner. We believe that driver Hopkins lived at 1 Spring Villas, Churchfields. The original photograph carries the caption 'Star of the West when all the rest are out'.

*Opposite:* SALISBURY OLD SHED, BEFORE THE FIRST WORLD WAR. Foreman Head Shunter Millard stands on the foot plate of engine No. 693 which is believed to be a Dugald Drummond '0-6-0' locomotive. This class became one of the workhorses of the London & South Western Railway. This particular machine was manufactured in 1897 at Nine Elms in London. Note the water arm to the left of the tender. Salisbury Old Shed is thought to have been situated near Fisherton House Lunatic Asylum (later the Old Manor Hospital).

MEMBERS OF SALISBURY CAMERA CLUB AT THE RAILWAY STATION ENTRANCE IN 1910. Wilfred A. Chaplin was the organiser of this particular railway excursion, and this is one of several photographs he took while out 'on safari' with his colleagues. He was a very keen amateur photographer who appears to have had quite a following at a time when photography was still a craft generally followed by professionals and the better off. It was an expensive hobby. Some years ago, Peter Daniels was fortunate enough to acquire a number of Mr Chaplin's prints and negatives, and they are now secure for future generations to enjoy. The bearded gentleman, standing on the extreme right in the station entrance, is believed to be Harry Medway, who was the Mayor of Salisbury in 1922.

READY FOR A RACING START AT SALISBURY RAILWAY STATION IN 1912! Here we can see a number of soldiers disembarking on platform two. They are men of the 9th Hampshire (Cycle) Regiment who had arrived in the city by train and, having offloaded their bicycles, they were about to set off and pedal their way to Sling Plantation camp at Bulford. Their regimental summer manoeuvres continued from 7-12 September. Notice the man with the oil can on the right and the nurse on the left. Another picture of the event has been reproduced on page 119.

THE SALISBURY BRANCH OF THE NATIONAL UNION OF RAILWAYMEN. This beautifully embroidered banner was rediscovered in 1988 having been found in a storeroom at Salisbury Station. It had been left there very many years earlier and as time passed by it was forgotten. The banner was ceremoniously unfurled in the Market Place on 21 July 1917 by the Mayor, Councillor Mr James Macklin. On the following day, it was paraded through the streets of Salisbury. We believe this photograph records that event. On the side of the banner facing us we can see a railwayman, a docker and a miner. On the reverse side a branch secretary is shown paying money to a widow and orphans.

A PHOTO OPPORTUNITY FOR A DOZEN SALISBURY RAILWAYMEN. Some of the names of these locomotive workers are still familiar around the city today. In the back row stand Messrs Elliott, Baker and Sampson, and in the middle row we can see Hall, Grantham, Minns, Howe, and Stoodley. In front are knelt Messrs Pope, Batchelor, Webbsell, and Pitman. Although undated, the photograph would appear to have been taken before the time of the Second World War.

THE MARKET HOUSE RAILWAY, SALISBURY, 1906. The Salisbury & Market House Company inaugurated this building on 24 May 1859. With the opening of the London & South Western Railway station at Fisherton in the same year, a full-gauge track to this point brought the railway right into the centre of the city. It is to Salisbury's credit that, when the Market House was converted into Salisbury Divisional Library, many features of this handsome building were preserved.

THE GREAT WESTERN RAILWAY STATION AT SALISBURY. Designed by Isambard Kingdom Brunel, the GWR terminus was one of the great engineer's usual type of all-over roofed stations. It was opened in June 1856. When the London and South Western Railway Company rebuilt its station, a subway was installed even though a footbridge (just coming into view on the left) had been constructed in 1860 to provide a link with the GWR station. The GWR terminus closed in 1932, but goods continued to be handled there for a further thirty years. The old building is now listed and can still be seen near Fisherton railway bridge, although the all-over canopy has long since disappeared.

A GREAT WESTERN RAILWAY MOTOR DELIVERY LORRY, 1910. This Swiss-made Orion petrol-driven commercial vehicle was originally carrying passengers around the capital as part of the London General Omnibus Company fleet. Later on, it was acquired by Victor James Blew of Milford Street, Salisbury, who was the local haulage agent for the Great Western Railway. After removal of the old bus bodywork, a drop-sided float body was fitted, and on 14 May 1909 the vehicle was allocated the Wiltshire registration mark 'AM-1411'. It can be seen here that the lorry carried sacks of coal but we know from other photographs that furniture removals and general parcel-carrying work was also undertaken. A wooden container body was lifted on and off the float body for that purpose.

THE GREAT WESTERN RAILWAY STATION AT FISHERTON, BEFORE THE SECOND WORLD WAR. It was in June 1956 that Great Western trains started to link Salisbury with Bristol and South Wales. Yet problems remained for passengers from the south of England. Travellers from Southampton, for example, had to leave the London and South Western Railway station at Milford and find their way across the City. Three years later, however, the problem was solved when the L&SWR extended their line through a tunnel under Bishop's Down into a new through station adjacent to the one shown here.

THE RAILWAY DISASTER AT SALISBURY, 1906. This was the scene on Fisherton Railway Bridge following the most horrific accident the city had ever experienced. At 1.57a.m. on 1 July 1906 the boat train, or American Special, was derailed on the eastern approach to Salisbury. As it entered the station, the Drummond L12 locomotive (No. 421) was travelling at an estimated 67mph as opposed to the maximum permitted speed of 30mph. The express overturned on an eight-chain curve, crashing into a stationary milk train that was standing on the down line. Sadly, twenty-eight people lost their lives, many of whom were Americans who had arrived at Plymouth on the *SS New York*. In this picture we can see the wreckage of several carriages being removed by crane. Windsor Road and the London Hotel come into view in the background. By Monday afternoon all train services through Salisbury were back to normal – an astounding achievement!

THE DAMAGED MILK TRAIN LOCOMOTIVE AT SALISBURY, 1 JULY 1906. Amongst the fatalities were the fireman and guard of the milk train and the driver and fireman of the boat train. Ironically, the guard of the milk train had swapped duties with a friend who had wanted to go shopping with his wife. A number of rooms at Salisbury Station were turned into temporary mortuaries after the crash and railway staff had the unenviable task of assisting grief-stricken relatives.

THE FUNERAL OF A BOAT TRAIN CASUALTY, JULY 1906. Here we can see a funeral cortège leaving the station from where it slowly proceeded to Salisbury Cathedral. The deceased was the Reverend Edward King of Toronto who had travelled to England on the SS New York to attend a special service at St Paul's Cathedral. On the left of the photograph we can see a few forgotten features from Salisbury's past: The brick wall in the foreground once surrounded the stationmaster's house. There were also three large wooden gates that occasionally sealed off the South Western Road entrance to the railway station site. Passing through the gates on this particular occasion was one of Robert Stokes' horse-drawn vans, which was probably out delivering orders from Stokes Tea and Coffee Warehouse in Canal. Coming into view in the distance are a number of railway outbuildings that have also long since disappeared.

A PEACEFUL SCENE AT SALISBURY STATION IN THE 1920s. In these modern times we are all used to seeing posters, signs and product displays wherever we go. Even police forces are now carrying brightly coloured sponsorship graphics on certain types of vehicle. The need to create public awareness of one's product or service is nothing new, however. As can be seen in this picture, there were literally dozens of posters, displays and directional signs dotted around this area of Salisbury Station. On the left stands the WH Smith & Son kiosk above which is displayed an advertisement for the Cathedral Hotel. There are also numerous point-of-sale posters for the popular magazines of the day. On the other side of the station exit are fixed a variety of enamel panels promoting Whitbreads Beer, the County Hotel, and St Martin's School at Sidmouth. There is also a sign for the stationmaster's office. Among the other highlighted products are International Stores, Mazawattee Tea, Dymond Estate Agents of Bideford, Cocks Leather, Metropole Hotel at Padstow, Petter oil engines, and J.W. Walker clocks. Walkers, incidentally, were official suppliers of clocks to the London & South Western Railway Company. It is one of their timepieces that we can see in the centre of this picture.

A PHOTO OPPORTUNITY AT MILFORD GOODS STATION, BEFORE 1930.
Unfortunately, the names of these individuals have not been recorded, but we do recognise one
face, that of Thomas Burden, who stands third from the right in the back row. He was a
weighbridge attendant. On the extreme left we can just see one of Chaplin & Company's horse-
drawn vans. They were railway agents, carriers and furniture removers who were situated not
far from the goods station. Chaplin's link with the L&SWR is legendary. His financial
experience, business acumen and contacts transformed a somewhat dysfunctional railway
company into a considerable force that was able to meet its great competitor, the Great
Western Railway, head on. Chaplin later became MP for Salisbury.

MILFORD GOODS STATION, SALISBURY, 1952. Milford Station functioned as a terminus
from 1857 until 2 May 1859 when the main Salisbury Station was opened. The building you
see here had a mixed career. Originally an engine shed, it was later used as the transfer shed.
At the time of this photograph it had become a store.

GWR DEAN GOODS TRAIN AT SALISBURY DURING THE SECOND WORLD WAR.
This was one of William Dean's standard '0-6-0' locomotives designed for the Great Western
Railway. Many of them were taken over by the government for military service, mainly
overseas, at the time of the First and Second World Wars. In a few instances, the same engine
was called up for service in both conflicts. This picture is believed to have been taken during
the early years of the Second World War and may have been one of three Dean Goods engines
that were used to haul the huge railway guns to Bulford Camp. They had probably stopped at
Salisbury to take on water. Unfortunately, the names of the soldiers have not been recorded.

A GANG OF SHUNTERS AT SALISBURY EAST STATION YARD, JULY 1947. This photograph was taken by Jack Barker, who was also a member of the gang. Foreman Alvis stands on the left (sadly no longer with us) then comes Stan Everett, J. Scott (deceased), an unidentified member of the gang, Driver Sanger (deceased), and nearest to the camera, Fireman Goodfellow. Behind them stands a Class Z '0-8-0' locomotive, No. 30957. The Salisbury East Station Yard is now derelict.

A DOWN TRAIN TO EXETER, SALISBURY, 1952. The 9a.m. from Waterloo is arriving at Salisbury Station on Wednesday 11 March, departing for Exeter at 10.54a.m. We are told that this is a very rare photograph. The diesel shown is a 1600hp Co-Co, which is one of three similar locomotives designed by H.G. Ivatt, the chief mechanical engineer of the LMS, in late 1945. British Rail had transferred it from the Euston and St Pancras routes to the southern region, where it remained until 1955.

SALISBURY SHED AT THE TWILIGHT OF STEAM. Here we can see 34100 *Appledore* and 34002 *Salisbury* standing outside the railway sheds. They are both Bulleid Light Pacifics, part of the slightly lighter edition of the Merchant Navy class. Built between 1945-49, they received these numbers under nationalisation. In 1956, some modifications were made to the running gear of the Merchant Navy class and their streamlined casing was removed (the original boxed-in appearance had led to them being nicknamed, rather unfairly, 'spam cans'!). Steam trains such as these were used on the London, Bournemouth and Weymouth lines until as recently as July 1967, when an abrupt conversion was made to electrification.

JOURNEY'S END AT SALISBURY STATION, 21 JULY 1962. This Class U1 '2-6-0' locomotive brings our journey through Salisbury's railway heritage to an end. It was built by R.E.L. Maunsell, during the years 1928-31, to a design of converted '2-6-4' Ts with a few minor modifications. This locomotive epitomises the days of steam.

# Two
# Around
# the Nadder Valley

THE DINING ROOM OF THE SHIP HOTEL IN MERE, BEFORE 1910. This popular inn, once the scene of cock fights, was the home of Sir John Coventry MP until 1682 (some believe that it was his banishment from court which led to the saying 'Sent to Coventry'). The Ship was first licensed as a coaching inn in the eighteenth century and it takes its name from the sailing ship badge of Johannes de Mere who founded a chantry in the church during the fourteenth century. When Frederick Holmes took this photograph, the proprietor of the hotel was Walter Harry Read, who was a carpenter by trade.

AN EDWARDIAN VIEW FROM THE SQUARE AT MERE. The clock tower was built on the site of the old market house where William Barnes, the poet, held his first school. When the market house reached a stage of serious decline in 1863, the Duchy of Cornwall demolished it and the clock tower was erected as a gift to the community. It can be seen that a rather untidy advertising hoarding had been attached to one side of the building. A mix of local and national posters was glued there, including an advertisement for John Walton's shops at Mere and Wilton. It seems rather odd for Mr Walton to have paid for advertising his local outlet on the posters; many of the shops in Mere belonged to him, including one to the right of the clock tower.

NORRIS'S FARM AT MERE IN THE EARLY TWENTIETH CENTURY. There are more than a dozen farms listed in Mere in the 1907-1911 editions of Kelly's Directory of Wiltshire, but this particular one is not included. If it had not been for the sign writing on the front of the hay cart we would never have identified the location. The wagon bulkhead carries the name of 'Matthew Norris, Mere – 1907'. A properly thatched square hayrick can be seen at the back with a new one being prepared to the left. Women and children were often expected to help the men on these occasions. William Norris of North Street took the photograph. We wonder if the families were related?

VICTIMS OF WAR, THE SALMON FAMILY AT MERE, 1915. Like many of their compatriots, the Salmons fled from Belgium ahead of the German occupation. They were one of two refugee families to reach Mere. Their clothing would suggest they were a fairly prosperous family, and they were able to stay in Tubbs House (a temperance hotel) in Castle Street for a number of years.

THE FIRST MERE MOTOR OMNIBUS, 1913. The service is believed to have been inaugurated on 8 January by Mr Rawlings of Hindon. Manufactured by the Scout Motor Company of Salisbury, the conveyance is believed to be Mere's first mechanised public transport system. Linking the town with Gillingham, it left the Square at 8a.m., 12.30p.m. and 3.30p.m. from May to September, and then with a reduced service during the winter months. Services were also run to Salisbury on market days via Hindon. In the background we see John Walton's ironmongery shop and to the right is the clock tower.

CORONATION DAY IN MERE, 22 JUNE, 1911. Characteristically, the people of Mere celebrated the coronation of their new King, George V, in great style. Many of the public, commercial and residential buildings were lavishly decorated in red, white and blue. The town's fire brigade turned out with their horse-drawn steam fire engine, which is believed to have been purchased from Shand Mason & Company, of Blackfriars Road, London in 1905. Captain A.L. Coward stands alongside the appliance. The firemen appear to be wearing 'Metro'-style helmets. This was out of character with other local brigades who still retained the old traditional type of ornate brass fire helmets as part of their uniform. Although its main features are hidden under a colourful display of flowers, the motor car has the characteristics of a Clement Talbot, which coincidentally leads us to look at the Talbot Inn standing in the background. Out of view to the left was situated the firehouse which is now an ambulance station.

*Opposite:* ERNEST WHITMARSH'S GARAGE, MERE, AT THE TIME OF THE FIRST WORLD WAR. Originally a blacksmiths, situated in Castle Street, this was a family business that had been in existence for 200 years. When the photograph was taken, Ernest Whitmarsh and his two brothers were running the business. One of their many activities was the production of shoes for army mules by a manufacturing process invented by their father. The forge and workshop was eventually demolished in 1967 to facilitate a road-widening scheme. At that time, the two remaining brothers retired.

THE GREEN AT STOURTON, BEFORE THE GREAT WAR. We are looking at a meeting of the South and West Wiltshire Hounds. Originally partly in Somerset since before the Norman Conquest, the village had belonged to the Roman Catholic Stourton family. In 1720, the estates were purchased by Henry Hoare, a wealthy banker from London. His beautiful house and gardens at Stourhead are now in the possession of the National Trust and are well worth a visit.

STOURTON, NEAR MERE, IN THE 1930s. Here we can see the estate village of the Hoare family, who lived in the house and beautiful gardens of Stourhead. To the right stands the Spread Eagle hotel, outside of which stand two Morris cars, a Wolseley and what would appear to be an American Hudson tourer. Their occupants were probably tourists, five of whom can be seen seated at the tables on the lawn. They are being served with refreshments. Coming into view further up the road is the Stourton Village Memorial Hall, formerly the inn stables. The conversion to a village club was carried out by the Hoare family 'in memory of those who fell in the Great War'. It is now a National Trust refreshment room.

THE STREET, EAST KNOYLE, 1912. The bottom end of Knoyle House, owned by the Seymour family, lies behind the archway on the right. Swan Cottage stands this side of it. In the middle of the road, close to the arch, can be seen a pony and trap which is believed to have been owned by Mr Hibberd of Tisbury. He published a great many picture postcards in the early years of the twentieth century, a number of which feature the pony and trap. It would appear that the carriage was used to good effect by adding character to what could otherwise have been a less interesting scene. On this particular occasion, the cart doubled as a warning to approaching vehicles that there was an obstacle around the corner. The photographer would have been standing in the middle of the road with a large tripod and camera. At times, his head was hidden under a black cloth, an item of equipment that all photographers used at that time. On the left of the picture stands the post office, which in earlier times had been the Black Horse Inn. Henry Burton was the postmaster, his family having arrived in the village in 1872. They are still represented in the village today.

KNOYLE HOUSE, 1908. The picture records a meeting of the South and West Wiltshire Hunt, which gathered in a field called Broadmead below the ha-ha of Knoyle House. To the left of the house stands Bell Cottage, which still has the bell outside its west end that was used to summon the Clouds Fire Brigade. Knoyle House belonged to the Seymour family until the end of the nineteenth century; it later became the home of the Dowager Lady Pembroke who founded the Beatrix Nursery Home there. The building was demolished in the 1950s.

THE FUNERAL OF CANON MILFORD AT EAST KNOYLE, 21 JUNE 1913. The school flag flew at half-mast on this sad occasion. The headmaster, Mr F.N. Barnes, can be seen standing in the school grounds paying his last respects. Canon Milford had been rector from 1865 to 1912. He and his wife had raised ten children during that long period. The village hall and the church lie beyond. The new rector, the Reverend William Neville, walks in front of the coffin, wearing a biretta.

CHURCH RAILS, EAST KNOYLE, 1909. Prominent in the centre of this picture is an unusual house, which has a peaked roof. This was 'The Enterprise', built by a retired innkeeper around 1880 and named after one of his pubs. After the publican's death, Canon Milford, the rector, was guardian to his orphaned daughter and placed her with 'a worthy widow' living along the Semley road. The church lies lower down to the right of the photograph.

EAST KNOYLE RECTORY IN THE 1930s. This is the medieval part of the larger rectory, to the right, which was built in 1799. In 1633, it was the residence of the Reverend Dr Wren, the father of Sir Christopher Wren. Christopher spent his early years here although he was born in a residence which later became Haslem's shop that was demolished in the 1870s. The conservatory to the left has now gone.

THE STREET, EAST KNOYLE, BEFORE THE FIRST WORLD WAR. On the immediate right we can see the Congregational chapel next to which stands the Manse and Jupe's School, which is now a private residence. Charles Jupe came from Mere and was a strong Congregationalist. Further down the road is a cottage called Summerlea and on the left, just out of view, is the old forge, which is now a garage. Tom Bath was the blacksmith when this picture was taken. By 1922, Albert Sully had become the smithy. The man sitting on the brick wall in the foreground of the picture was probably taking a break from his work. He may well have been a professional painter and decorator because he is clutching what appears to be a well-made paint scraper in his hand. The photographer probably asked him to sit there to add some life to the scene.

THE HIGH STREET, HINDON, JUST AFTER THE SECOND WORLD WAR. We are looking north towards the church of St John the Baptist, which replaced an earlier chapel-of-ease in 1871. The bishops of Winchester 'planted' Burgus Hindon early in the thirteenth century. It flourished, especially during the stagecoach era, but declined to village status when the railway later bypassed it. The trees shown in the picture were planted in 1863 by Sir Michael Shaw-Stewart to commemorate the wedding of the Prince of Wales (later King Edward VII). A variety of Morris and Austin cars are to be seen parked in the road.

AN AERIAL VIEW OF OLD WARDOUR CASTLE IN THE 1950s. The ruins of the old castle, unusually hexagonal in shape, are well hidden by the surrounding woodland. The castle, originally built by Lord John Lovell in 1397, was purchased by the Arundell family in 1547. Having lost control of the castle to the parliamentary forces during the Civil War, it was retaken by the 3rd Lord Arundell – but only by destroying the fabric of the castle in the process. New Wardour Castle was built to replace it as a home for the Arundells in 1776.

THE 'NEW' CHURCH OF SAINT LEONARD AT SEMLEY, 1897. A parish church has stood in this village since Norman times. From 1866, however, a new one had replaced the old, retaining the circular Norman font and a thirteenth-century effigy of a priest. In the Lady Chapel can be seen a beautiful stained glass window in memory of WPC Yvonne Fletcher, a native of the village, who was shot and killed in the Libyan Embassy Siege on 17 April 1984. The photograph was taken by Clement Osmond, of Salisbury, who was not only a skilled professional stonemason but also a gifted amateur photographer.

SCAMMELL'S GROCERY SHOP AND POST OFFICE AT LUDWELL, 1910. Albert Joseph Scammell was proprietor of the post office, bakery and general store at this time. His bakery lies out of view to the right of the shop. In the background of the picture stands Lansdowne Villa, the home of the Misses May and Maggie Gatehouse. Miss May was a Sunday school teacher at Saint John's Church, Charlton, another hamlet close by. On the extreme left can just be seen the tailor's shop, which was run by their brother Harold.

*Opposite:* SEMLEY RECTORY, 1910. The drawing room can be seen on the right of the rectory, which was built between 1735-60. The bay window and the west wing, which included the domestic quarters, were added around 1860. The Reverend Louis Kercheval Hilton was living there when this delightful picture was taken. Before 1914, the Slate Club Feast Day always commenced here with the Rector accompanying the parade to the church for a special service. After a sumptuous lunch at the Benett Arms everyone would return for tea and dancing on the lawn.

THE MAIDMENT FAMILY AND FRIENDS AT DONHEAD IN AROUND 1907. On the left of the picture we can see Elizabeth Maidment with her three daughters: Bertha (the eldest of twelve children), Flora, and Dolly. Elizabeth married James Maidment in 1901. The family walked to church every Sunday to attend two services. It was a round trip of three miles each time. James, who was head gardener at Donhead Hall from 1915 until his retirement forty years later, sang in the church choir. At home and in his allotment garden he grew enough produce to keep his family self-sufficient and to compete at the local show in Shaftesbury. He won hundreds of awards for his fine fruit and vegetables. He passed away in 1963 at the age of ninety-two.

DONHEAD LODGE, DONHEAD SAINT ANDREW, AT THE TIME OF THE FIRST WORLD WAR. A memorial tablet in the church is a fitting tribute to Captain John Cooke, who lived in this house. After a distinguished career, he was killed at an early stage of the Battle of Trafalgar. His ship, *Bellerophon*, later took Bonaparte to final captivity and death on Saint Helena. The house has been altered on many occasions over the years.

PYT HOUSE, HATCH, NEAR TISBURY, EARLY 1900s. This was the home of the Benett family from the thirteenth century until the middle of the twentieth century. The present building was redesigned by 'Long' John Benett in around 1801. It was the scene of one of the more violent manifestations of the Swing Riots in 1830, when John Benett tried unsuccessfully to prevent the destruction of his two threshing machines. The South and West Wiltshire Hunt was gathering on the lawn when Mr Holmes of Mere took this picture.

TISBURY HIGH STREET IN THE 1930s. The original picture has been described as 'Tisbury Cross', possibly named after the inn on the right or because it is the meeting point of several roads. It is not an official name. Next to the inn on the right were to be found the premises of Charles Alfred Walsh & Son, drapers. Although it is difficult to make out in the photograph, the two houses on the left stood on an island in the middle of the road. Frank Gatehouse's saddlery shop, later to become Pickford's hairdressing salon, lies behind the sign advertising Robert Wiltshire's motorcycle garage, which was situated behind the Cross Inn. In the centre of the picture we can see James Mould talking to Mrs Lambert, who lived in the Quarry Cottages. These are also to be found behind the pub.

CECIL MARSHALL'S FIRST CYCLE SHOP AT TISBURY, 1926. Cecil was born in Staverton in South Devon and he arrived in Tisbury in 1901 with his father, Uriah, who came to be gardener for the vicar. His interest in cycles and motorcyles (he took part regularly in the London to Exeter Motorcycle Rally) led to him starting his own business in this tiny shed attached to the Boot Inn in 1920. The inn burnt down in 1929 and the cycle shed with it. Cecil then took over the nearby shop which his son, David, still runs today.

*Opposite:* THE OVERHOUSE LAUNDRY DELIVERY VAN, TISBURY, 1903. The Benett Stanfords of Pyt House started the laundry in the 1880s. Situated in The Avenue, it was originally intended for their personal use. However, demand soon grew and by the beginning of the twentieth century, the laundry had developed into a flourishing business serving much of the surrounding area. Their first motorised delivery vehicle was a Wolseley, pictured here at the workshops of the Warminster Motor Company. The vehicle had been fitted with a cumbersome canvas-covered body that greatly overhung the back axle, giving it a completely unbalanced appearance. The wheels were made of wood in the traditional manner with solid rubber bands at the rear and cushioned tyres at the front.

40

T.P. LILLY'S TISBURY STONEYARD IN 1894. Situated behind the station, the yard received stone for finishing before onward transportation by rail. There were numerous open-cast quarries in the Tisbury area. Mr E.E. Gething, who ran the Chilmark Stone Quarry, is pictured in front and to the right of this group. He wears a pork-pie hat. Among the other stonemasons can be seen Bill Gauler, Fred Rixon, Fred Turner, Ernest Parsons, Edward Green, Charles Gauler, Joe Snook, Henry Rixon, James Rixon, and Herbert Rixon. Thomas Parks Lilly was the yard proprietor and James Rixon was the foreman.

S.G. BAKER'S BUTCHERS SHOP IN TISBURY HIGH STREET, 1925. G. Baker, T. Lush, R. Green and W. Lloyd are pictured here in front of the shop with a magnificent display of meat and poultry. There would appear to be three types of printed certificates shown on the display: First and Champion – Coplesgove; First and Reserve Champion – Crewke; and First Prize – Maiden Heifer. Gil Baker, the proprietor, is shown on the left.

A CRICKET MATCH AT TISBURY, 9 JUNE 1906. This match, played between teams from Tisbury and Salisbury, took place in a field adjacent to the River Nadder. In the middle of the picture we can see a row of trees which mark the line of a new road from Chicksgrove. Today the trees are fully matured beeches. In the centre in the distance is a house that was, for a time, the vicarage. The chapel to its right is Zion Hill, a Congregational chapel, which for some years now has been closed awaiting re-development. The message on the back of the original picture postcard reads: 'Going to win the next three matches and beat the record!'

THE FARM UNIT AT DUNWORTH SECONDARY SCHOOL, TISBURY, IN THE 1960s. At this time, it was still the policy of Wiltshire County Council to encourage the teaching of Rural Studies, as agricultural workers were still required. 'Bish' Bishop, the school caretaker from 1961-80 can be seen with the sheep on the left. Audrey Scott and Sheila Wallace (gardens and stock assistants) are shown with the cattle. Roy Frankland was the headmaster at that time. The school became the Nadder Middle School in 1983.

THE FAMILY GROCER'S SHOP IN SWALLOWCLIFFE, 1906. Kelly's Directories of Wiltshire informs us that Thomas Francis Spencer was the village grocer and linen-draper between 1899 and the mid-1920s. He can be seen here standing at the entrance to the shop, which he ran with the assistance of his wife and six daughters, five of whom are believed to be shown here. The shop was situated on the corner of High Street in close proximity to the church. At the time that Charlie May, of Porton, took this photograph there would appear to have been a Sunlight Soap promotion taking place; the shop window is packed with display boxes of that particular product. Also to be seen are packets of Birds Custard Powders, boxes of Cadbury's chocolates, tins of Peek Frean biscuits, boxes of Red Swan matches, and cartons of Lifebuoy soap.

THE MANOR HOUSE, SWALLOWCLIFFE, 1906. The farmer, William Keevil, was living here at that time. On his retirement in the following year, the villagers presented him with an illuminated address as a token of their appreciation for all the kindness he had shown to them throughout the nineteen years of his residency. During the early 1920s, Captain Henry Cavendish, a cousin of the Duke of Devonshire, bought the property and added the stylish north wing that we see today.

CHILMARK VILLAGE IN 1914. The picture was taken in The Street. To the right lies the small stream that rises close by and feeds into the Nadder just south of the village. To the left, behind the wall, stands Chilmark House and beyond the pony and trap are situated Chilmark Manor and the lane known as Barberry, which leads to the parish church of St Margaret of Antioch. Chilmark Quarry produced much of the stone for the churches, houses and fine mansions in this part of the county as well as some for the cathedrals at Old and New Sarum.

CHILMARK AT THE DAWN OF THE TWENTIETH CENTURY. This picture was taken at the bottom of Becketts Lane. We are looking towards the parish church of St Margaret of Antioch at the top of a steep lane known as Barberry. The church name is unusual and is believed to have been given by returning Crusaders. The lych-gate, through which the churchyard is entered, was a memorial to Emma Lindsell, who was killed when thrown from her pony and trap. The building on the left is Chilmark Manor.

THE BLACK HORSE INN AT TEFFONT MAGNA IN THE 1930s. The People's Refreshment House Association (PRHA) managed the inn at that time. It was not their only public house in the area; they also held the license for the Bell Inn at Wilton. Both of the cars shown here are tourer models with fold-down hoods. The one on the left is a Rover. The other car is a rarer type; possibly a Talbot. The Black Horse has been closed for some considerable time and its future remains uncertain.

DINTON BRICK, TILE AND POTTERY WORKS IN THE EARLY 1900s. Situated off Bratch Lane, this local industry was opened by the Pembroke Estate in 1904. It catered for the increasing needs of the building trade and proved to be extremely versatile, embracing a pottery works and three large brick kilns. Drainpipes, faience, garden ornaments and tiles were made here in addition to several types of house-building bricks.

THE WYNDHAM ARMS HOTEL, DINTON, AT THE TIME OF THE GREAT WAR. The coming of the railway in 1859 brought about the need for a hotel to be built close to the station. The Wyndham Arms was opened around 1860 by William Wyndham, of Dinton House (now a National Trust property known as Philips House). A large stable block was erected to enable local farmers to attend Salisbury Market by train. As many as fifty vehicles could be assembled here on a market day. The hotel is now a private residence. The photographer had 'borrowed' two soldiers to liven up his picture; they are an Australasian sergeant (left) and a British Military Police officer.

COMPTON HOUSE AND ST MICHAEL'S CHURCH, COMPTON CHAMBERLAYNE, 1868. This beautiful mansion, set among sweeping parkland, lies at the end of the small village. It was originally built in Tudor Gothic style in 1550 by Sir Edward Penruddocke with the elegant spring-fed lake added much later. In the following century, it was remodelled in the Early Stuart style with dining room carvings from the workshops of Grinling Gibbons. The estate was to remain with the Penruddocke family for nearly four centuries. This 'carte de visite' style of photograph is among the earliest images in the book. It was produced by Edwin Macy, of the Wiltshire Photographic Rooms at Town Mill House in St Thomas's Square, Salisbury.

A NEW ZEALAND EXPEDITIONARY FORCE AMBULANCE AT FOVANT IN 1918. Supplied by the Ministry of War for government use, this 20hp Daimler was allocated the Wiltshire registration number AM 7136 on 16 November 1916. The plate was issued by the vehicle taxation office in Trowbridge. The dark grey coloured ambulance was garaged and maintained at the New Zealand Reserve Group Headquarters at Sling Plantation, Bulford. It was put to good use carrying wounded and sick soldiers around the Salisbury Plain camps. The ambulance driver is Private Merle, who thoughtfully scribbled a message to Vera, which included the following comment: 'This is my car, what do you think of it? It is lovely to drive.'

A REFRESHMENT HUT AT FOVANT CAMP IN JULY 1922. With the outbreak of war in 1914, Fovant was transformed into a bustling military centre, as the need for training camps for British and Commonwealth troops became urgent. Throughout the years of the First World War, many thousands of soldiers were stationed in the area and the last ones did not leave until 1920. Civilian contractors were then employed to dismantle the camps and many of the army huts were sold later to function as village halls and temporary houses. A number of them can still be found in the county today. Here we can see a group of workmen enjoying a welcome break from their labours.

THE FRANCIS FAMILY OF BARFORD ST MARTIN. Harry Francis is pictured here in 1900 with his wife Sarah Lot (née Hardiman) and their children. Emily stands at the back of the group and her shy little sister Rose can be seen in the foreground. We do not know the names of the two boys; do you recognise them? The family lived in a cottage off the main road near the Dragon Inn (which later changed to the Green Dragon Inn).

BARFORD ST MARTIN FOOTBALL CLUB ANNUAL OUTING, 1923. This event took place just prior to the club's best season, when they won the Nadder Valley Cup. Among the players was Joe Chalke, a spar and hurdle maker, then aged twenty-eight, who continued to play for the club until his early forties, winning several medals in competitive matches. Pictured here in front of the Green Dragon inn at Barford St Martin are six charabancs from the fleet of Rowland Motor Coaches, Salisbury. A Sunbeam (HR 7714) stands to the left; next in line is a Dennis (HR 128); then come four Leylands, which include TB 5023, AF-2292 and B-5517.

# *Three*

# Around
# the Wylye Valley

EAST STREET, WARMINSTER, AT THE DAWN OF THE TWENTIETH CENTURY. On the left of this photograph we can see the premises of G. Bush & Company, a very versatile business which embraced a complete house furnishers, cabinet makers, upholsterers, carpet and bedding makers, and an undertakers. A block of private residences has recently been built on the site. The bay-windowed property opposite, now a bookshop, was at that time the offices of Albert Long (architect), William Morgan (brewer), and the Warminster Gas Company. Also to be found on that side of the street was Montalvo's Refreshment Rooms (of which Charles William Estavan Montalvo was proprietor), and the Mason's Arms Inn (of which Frederick James Shepherd was licensee).

WARMINSTER IN RED, WHITE AND BLUE, 23 JUNE 1909. This was the scene in George Street on the day that the Prince and Princess of Wales (the future King George V and Queen Mary) travelled from Westbury Station to Lord Bath's home at Longleat. The people of Warminster treated the occasion like a holiday, and many companies and individuals decorated their homes and buildings with colourful displays of flags, bunting and ribbons. The town band was set up at Portway. Unfortunately, heavy rain set in and the Royal party passed through in a closed carriage.

JOHN MICHAEL FLEETWOOD
FULLER, 1906. John Fuller was
Warminster's MP from 1900-1911, and he
lived at Jaggards in Corsham. The eldest
son of G.P. Fuller of Neston Park,
Corsham, he was born there on 21
October 1864. After completing his
education at Winchester College and
Christ Church, Oxford, he began a
distinguished career. This included
becoming a DC to the Viceroy of India
in 1894-5, and promotion to Major in
the Royal Wilts Imperial Yeomanry
from 1900. He was a Justice of the
Peace for Wiltshire, an Alderman of
Wiltshire County Council and Vice
Chairman of the Roads and Bridges
Committees. He travelled extensively
in Asia, South Africa, North and South
America and Australasia, where he
became Governor of Victoria from 1911-
14. His marriage to Norah Jacintha (the
second daughter of C.N.P. Phipps, of
Chalcot, Westbury, who was formerly an
MP for Westbury) produced three
daughters: Bridget, Patience, and Maude.

A PHOTO OPPORTUNITY AT MARKET PLACE, WARMINSTER IN 1906. In the centre
background can be seen the campaign offices for the 1906 General Election in which John
Fuller stood as the candidate for the Liberal party. He was successfully re-elected as the MP for
the Westbury constituency by 5,264 votes to 3,788 against his component Lord Dunsany. The
group is gathered around a Humber motorcar that was operating on a Wiltshire motor trader's
registration plate: AM 6 DS. On the right can be seen Luke's plumbers and picture-framing
shop at 9 High Street (of which Herbert James Luke was proprietor).

THE WARMINSTER MOTOR COMPANY GARAGE IN GEORGE STREET, BEFORE 1910. The company was founded by Lewis Claude Wilcox. His father was a local doctor. The garage was built in 1905 on the site of the old Castle Inn. The showroom was in front, with workshops behind. In 1935, the company was described as a motor engineers, official repairers to the AA and RAC, wireless engineers, and radio specialists. The building was demolished in the early 1960s along with Castle Laundry and Carr's Garage. Octagon Garage occupies the site today. The cars shown in the picture were very rare types even in those days. The one parked in the side entrance is a 14hp Beaufort tonneau (AM 140) registered to Hutton & Company. The large open car in the centre of the picture is a Corre 24hp green-coloured four-seater that was allocated the Wiltshire registration mark AM 905 in August 1906.

SUTTON VENY CROSSWAY, 1915. The original photograph was produced by Alfred Vowles, who we believe was the Sutton Veny camp photographer. He had engaged the services of a few passers-by to add some interest to this scene that he describes as 'The Dangerous Crossway at Sutton Veny'. We are looking towards Norton Road at the top of the village. Among the group of 'extras' can be seen two soldiers from a Scottish regiment and two young lads. We wonder if the old gentleman with the horse and wagon is Isaac Norris, the Sutton Veny carrier?

*Opposite:* HATCHET CORNER, MARKET PLACE, WARMINSTER, AT THE TIME OF THE GREAT WAR. We are looking towards East Street with Station Road turning off to the left. In front of you can be seen the Warminster Post Office, which stands on the site of an old inn called 'The Hatchet'. Originally built as the Somerset & Wiltshire Savings Bank, the post office was opened in 1903. Partly hidden by the stationery Ford car is a marble fountain that was erected by William Morgan in 1892 in memory of his wife Catherine. It was moved some years ago and can now be found in the Lake and Pleasure Gardens. The post office closed in 1995.

THE GROUNDS OF SUTTON VENY MILITARY HOSPITAL, 1915. The hospital was situated at Greenhill House, which had been taken over by the Australian YMCA. Apart from being a hospital and convalescent centre, the house provided numerous activities to create a 'home-from-home' atmosphere for the Australian troops. The soldier on the extreme right stands at the door of the Administrator's office, and two of his colleagues are to be seen alongside a Daimler ambulance that carries OHMS markings (On His Majesty's Service). A close-up photograph of a similar machine can be seen on page 48.

THE LOCK-UP AT HEYTESBURY. The original picture postcard is described as 'the old prison'. These inhospitable buildings were more commonly known as 'blind houses' because of their lack of windows. They were used for drunks and other miscreants who required temporary overnight accommodation until their appearance before the local magistrate the following morning. Similar buildings can still be seen in other parts of South Wiltshire, including Shrewton.

BERNARD WRIGHT WITH HIS TRIUMPH MOTORBIKE AT IMBER POST OFFICE.
The post office was built early in the twentieth century. It was one of the few buildings to be
seen on the north of the main road through the village. There was a 'Postman's Path' from
Codford which the postman walked to deliver the mail in the morning, taking the outgoing
letters with him in the afternoon. John Carter had been the sub-postmaster since the post office
first opened and he was still there at the outbreak of the Second World War. Bernard, who lived
at Ladywell, looks at ease sitting on this sturdy Triumph motorcycle and sidecar. The
registration number NB 6515 was issued in Manchester in 1919.

ELIZA AND JAMES DANIELS OF IMBER. Both were born in 1855 – James at Imber and Eliza at Tilshead. James, who died on 17 February 1920, was an agricultural labourer. His wife passed away six years later. For many years, the couple lived at No. 7 High Street. Both are laid to rest in the Baptist Chapel graveyard at Imber.

IMBER HIGH STREET IN THE EARLY TWENTIETH CENTURY. The cottages shown here are typical of the domestic buildings to be seen in the village at that time. Many of them were thatched and they had whitewashed walls. Here we are looking at a group of cottages on the left of the road heading towards Warminster. You can see the well outside John Cruse's cottage, down which he is reputed to have thrown the china and silver from the table following an argument. A winter bourne, known as Imber Dock, lies to the right of this pastoral scene, and Tinker's Barn, owned by Sydney Dean, is viewed in the distance.

THE PEOPLE OF IMBER CELEBRATING KING GEORGE V's CORONATION IN 1911. The young ones are lined up to have their photograph taken before sitting down to enjoy a Coronation dinner in the Jubilee Barn (named after Queen Victoria's Jubilee). This can be seen on the left of the picture. The tower of St Giles Church comes into view in the distance. Bernie and Gladys Wright are among the children, who include Enos Matthews, Fred Dean, Joel Cruse, Tom Dean, Sidney Dean (wearing a boater hat), and Kate Dean.

CHITTERNE FROM THE HILL, 1920s. The original photograph carries the mark of Alfred Burgess of Market Lavington. Here, his camera was pointing towards the north of the village of Chitterne. In the middle ground we can clearly see the white painted walls of Woodbine Cottages, which are now combined into one. This is where the village policeman lived. The church of All Saints and St Mary's comes into view in the distance, and Elm Farm occupies the foreground. A steam-driven threshing machine would appear to have been abandoned in the farmyard. It looks like it has been left standing for some time.

THE KING'S HEAD INN, CHITTERNE, BEFORE THE FIRST WORLD WAR. This nineteenth-century hostelry can be seen on the Warminster Road, close to the turning to Codford St Mary. The landlord at the time of this photograph was George Henry Burgess. Despite its remoteness on the Plain, the inn remains a popular meeting place for the community and passing traffic. The sign above the door states: 'The Kings Head. George Burgess, Licensed Retailer of Tobacco, Wines and Spirits. Comfortable Accommodation and Good Stabling'.

THE HIGH STREET, CODFORD ST MARY, BEFORE 1908. On the immediate right can be seen the yard of Doughty & Simper, who were builders and cycle dealers. The large house further down on the right, 65 High Street, was the residence of the Minty family. Mrs Minty had a miraculous escape one day in 1944 when the house was knocked down by a tank. George Spiller lived in the house on the left; he worked for David Norris, the village baker. A snapshot of Norris's delivery van has been reproduced on the opposite page.

NORRIS'S MORRIS AT CODFORD ST MARY. Norris's Steam Bakery was to be found at 76 The High Street. David Norris had taken on the business after the First World War, having served previously in the Devonshire Regiment (despite having come from Hampshire!). During the Second World War, he was still active in the area, serving tea and buns to the British troops. He used to cook turkey for the American 3rd Armoured Division for Christmas and Thanksgiving. In this picture, David can be seen out on the rounds with the firm's Morris bread van. In the 1960s, he sold up and retired to Poole.

CODFORD ST PETER RAILWAY STATION, AFTER THE FIRST WORLD WAR. There was a time, before 1954, when this GWR line between Salisbury and Warminster had numerous stations. Opened in 1857, Codford Station was particularly busy at the time of the two world wars, supplying materials and men to the army camps of the Wylye Valley. Unusually, in this picture, the passengers appear to have priority over the train. The line was closed to passenger traffic in 1955 but the lines continued to carry freight trains for another five years.

THE FLOODS AT CODFORD ST MARY, JANUARY 1915. These two ladies with their dog look as though they have nowhere left to go. The winter of 1914-15 in South Wiltshire was one of the worst on record at that time. Many soldiers who were sleeping under canvas on the Plain became seriously ill or died through pneumonia and other respiratory problems. At Codford, where the Chitterne Brook meets the River Wylye, there were often problems with flooding during the winter months.

HAROLD TALBOT'S ARMY STORES AT CODFORD ST MARY. This shop with a galvanised roof might be described as a general store as it supplied a wide range of domestic products during the First World War, both to the villagers and the local troops. It lay at the junction of Codford High Street and the Chitterne Road. A sign on the wall to the left gives a warning that the bridge at Codford St Mary is unsafe for large engines to cross. During the Second World War, a popular café known as The Milk Bar was built on this site. It was frequently damaged by tanks turning out of the Chitterne Road. The cottages lying back next to it are still known as Milk Bar Cottages. The building seen further up on the left was, at one time, a branch of Lloyds Bank.

THE HIGH STREET, CODFORD ST MARY, AT THE TIME OF THE FIRST WORLD WAR. The building on the immediate right has been a general store on several occasions in the twentieth century – and is such today. Further down the road on the other side, where the recreation field is now situated, we can see a row of temporary shops that provided goods and services to the troops encamped in the area during the Great War. They included H.G. Stratton's Grocery & Provisions Stores, and the YMCA. One of these so-called temporary buildings, which remained until recently, was a village hall known as the Codford Club.

A POPULAR MEETING PLACE AT CODFORD, 1935. The footbridge lay at a point near the junction of the Chitterne Brook with the River Wylye at Codford St Mary. Mothers with children would often meet here for a gossip. The young ladies in this picture are believed to have been brought from London for a holiday by a local benevolent society.

63

THE MANOR HOUSE, BAPTON, 1909. This lovely house, situated near Stockton, originates from the seventeenth century, or earlier, with later extensions. The materials for the addition on the right came from the old Wylye railway station, following its closure. Among the many interesting owners of the manor was Sir Cecil Chubb, who purchased Stonehenge from the Antrobus Estate at Amesbury in 1915 and presented it to the nation three years later.

THE VILLAGE HIGH STREET, WYLYE, 1911. We are looking north with the post office (on the immediate right) which would have been quite new at that time. The Bell, a late-seventeenth-century coaching inn, can be seen further down the road. Beyond that is the Malt House with the Wyvern Hall attached, and finally the gable end of the mill. On the left stands James Pretty's butchers shop, Ethel Place, and Bell Cottage. The poplar trees, at the end, mark the passage of the ford across the River Wylye. The children would have come from the National School, which is out of view to the right. The picture, produced by R Wilkinson & Co., of Trowbridge, was published and sold by Frank Barter of Wylye. He would seem to have been a busy chap. Among other things he was a baker, a grocer, provisions merchant, a publisher, and an oil and petrol merchant.

WYLYE VILLAGE BEPORE 1910. Here we are looking north down the High Street. James Pretty's butchers shop can be seen on the immediate left. An iron rail was fitted under the canopy of his shop upon which joints of meat were hung. Although the building survives, it now forms part of Ethel Court. Hubert Colbourn, who died recently, worked in the shop as a young man. On the opposite side of the High Street we can see the church lych-gate that was erected in 1885 in memory of the Reverend J.S. Stockwell, a former rector, and his wife. The large building on the right is the Bell, a late-seventeenth-century coaching inn with a drapery and haberdashery shop standing next to it. The Malt House and Wyvern Hall come into view in the distance.

MECHANISED FARMING AT LITTLE LANGFORD IN THE 1920s. Henry Andrews, who farmed here in the latter half of the nineteenth century, invented the Andrews' Patent Sack Lifter, an example of which can be seen at Farmer Giles' Farmstead at Teffont Magna. In this picture we are looking at a typical farming scene in the Wylye Valley before the First World War, with a straw elevator preparing a stack. The young lad on the right guides the horse in a circular motion which turns a wheel and a drive belt that is connected to the elevator. This is real horse power!

A TEAM OF AGRICULTURAL WORKERS AT EAST CLYFFE FARM, STEEPLE LANGFORD, 1913. Henry Andrews, of Little Langford Farm, purchased East Clyffe Farm from Lord Ashburton in 1909. The family have continued to farm it ever since. This picture shows Grace Andrews (in the front) with a group of labourers from the farm, just before the outbreak of the First World War. We wonder who the little boy was in the centre of the picture? East Clyffe Farm was one of the last in the valley to work with horses.

THE PELICAN INN AT STAPLEFORD, BEFORE 1911. There have been quite a number of licensees who have had their name on the sign above the door since the nineteenth century. The numerous editions of Kelly's Directory of Wiltshire list these details. The landlord in 1848 was Thomas Becket, followd by Sarah Bennett in 1856, John Polden in 1859, Richard Perrott between 1867-75, George Jukes between 1880-85, Henry Thring in 1890, and Edwin Ward in 1899. At the time of this photograph, the innkeeper was George Hooper, who held the position between 1903-11, followed by Arthur Ernest Blanchard in 1915, Richard W. Judd in 1920, and finally Sidney Kilhams who seems to have survived as landlord until the 1950s.

OAKAPPLE DAY AT GREAT WISHFORD, AFTER THE SECOND WORLD WAR. The event would seem to have been staged in the 1950s. The Oakapple Day celebrations were much grander affairs in those days. Bartlett's Fun Fair was set up in the fair field on this particular occasion, and we can see one of their delivery vans parked behind the crowd in the centre of the picture. Coming into view on the far edge of the field are the traditional 'High Flyer' swinging boats. In the foreground are three competitors who took part in the Adult Fancy Dress contest. The young lady on the left adopted the theme of a once popular BBC programme called *Any Questions?* 'Is it Fact or Fiction?, Is it Useful?, Is it Alive?, Does it Move?, Is it Male or Female?, Is it Famous?, Can you Eat it?, Can you Wear it?, How many Legs does it have?, Is it in England?' These are her questions and we have one for you too: Who are these people?

SOUTH NEWTON NATIONAL SCHOOL, 1898. The school and a residence for the master and mistress are believed to have been built in the 1850s. The school was designed to accommodate up to eighty children, although at the time of this picture only around fifty pupils were attending. The longest serving headmaster would seem to have been Joseph Mason, who is probably the gentleman seen here on the left of the group.

SOUTH NEWTON WATER MILL, BEFORE 1908. This mill is among the earliest recorded in the Wylye Valley, and it is one of two mentioned in the Domesday Book. Standing at the southern end of the village, it was once much larger. We are looking at the millpond behind the mill with the miller, James Garner, standing in front. The eel-stage on the left was thatched at that time, later to be replaced by a corrugated tin roof. Most of the eels went to the Billingsgate Fish Market in London.

THE PRIDE AND JOY OF A SOUTH NEWTON FARMER. Built at the Scout Motor works in Churchfields Road, Salisbury, this 18/22hp car was delivered to John George Poigndestre Swanton of Manor Farm, South Newton. Recorded with chassis number 1075, the vehicle was allocated the Wiltshire registration mark AM-1587 on 8 March 1910. The bodywork of this smart-looking conveyance was hand-painted green and its wooden wheels were yellow. To add that touch of class, thin black lines were painted on the wings and on the spokes of the wheels. The upholstery was green leather. All external metal fixings were machined from brass and kept highly polished. The car was still in regular use in 1922, by which time it was owned by W. Street & Son, of East Wellow, Hampshire.

THE ROYAL OAK, GREAT WISHFORD, BEFORE 1910. The landlord at the time of this photograph was Albert Fox. The hostelry has always been central to the Oakapple Day celebrations, which have taken place traditionally on 29 May each year. The cottages you can see in the middle of the picture have now been demolished. An unusual feature of this picturesque village is the bread stones that are set into the wall of the churchyard. They record the price of bread over a period of many years, starting with three farthings per gallon in 1800. This picture-postcard view of Wishford was published by William Boning, of Wilton.

# Four

# Urchfont to Winterbourne Stoke

THE POND AT URCHFONT, 1906. Manor Farm lies to the immediate left of the pond with its yard and buildings opposite. The beech tree next to the farm was lost many years ago but the magnificent cedar can still be seen today. In the centre of the picture stands Mulberry House, the home of Robert Stone who was just one of numerous village doctors to have lived there. On the right, the Rectory comes into view, which at that time was the residence of Revd James Hill. The nearest fire brigade was stationed some distance away at Lavington, so the pond was particularly important when there was a fire in the village. Long dry summers often reduced the depth of the water, but in 1911 it dried up completely. This would appear to have been the only occasion when the Urchfont Brass Band played in the middle of the village pond!

GOODMAN'S SAWMILLS AT URCHFONT BOTTOM, 1910. The fact that this was originally a pub is indicated by three dark-green beer bottles that are still displayed in the wall beneath the eaves. A steam engine and saw were kept in the shed that stands on the left of the picture, behind which was constructed a saw-pit. We can see some very heavy timber planks piled up to the right. A stock of tree trunks ready for processing was always kept behind the cottage. When Charlie May took this particular photograph, he asked Mrs Goodman to stand in the doorway of the cottage with three of her children. Her husband, Ted eventually retired from the business in the mid-1930s, but none of his four sons would carry it on. This is now a private house.

AN OLD AGE PENSIONERS' WEDDING AT URCHFONT, BEFORE THE GREAT WAR. Unfortunately we have been unable to identify the newlyweds despite numerous enquiries having been made. Do you know who they are? The bride and groom are pictured here after the ceremony, which had presumably taken place in the local chapel or the church of St Michael and All Angels. The dark green, side-entry motor car was manufactured at the Scout Motor Company works in Salisbury in 1908. It was originally supplied to a motorist in Hampshire but on 18 June, 1910, the Southampton Motor Taxation office transferred ownership of the vehicle to James William Phipp & Sons of Maryport Street, Devizes. They were to use the car for private hire work, including weddings such as this.

URCHFONT POST OFFICE AND SHOP AT THE DAWN OF THE TWENTIETH CENTURY. The two people standing by the gate of their High Street premises are presumably the sub-postmaster William Payne and his wife, Mary Jane. The thatched house seen on the left became the site of Harry Fuller's Saddlery and, later on, it was a butcher's shop which sadly closed in 1998. The Lamb Inn is out of view to the right.

A FLOAT FROM THE URCHFONT CARNIVAL, 1923. This decorated boat wagon belonged to A.J. Hues of Rectory Farm in the nearby hamlet of Patney. We can see Dogtail Woods in the distance on the right of the picture. Local festivities nearly always took place in the grounds of Urchfont Manor, and the carnivals that were held in the 1920s always commenced their procession around the village from there too.

BROAD WELL, MARKET LAVINGTON, IN AROUND 1910. On the footbridge we can observe members of the Merrett family, who were blacksmiths in the village for very many years. The end of Beech House comes into view on the left. With three dipping wells and a pump, Broad Well provided a source of drinking water for many well-less residents – which at the time was about half the village. Consequently, it was a good place for a gossip. Mains water pipes were installed in the village in 1936.

MISS CHINNOCK'S SCHOOL AT MARKET LAVINGTON, BEFORE 1920. A teacher and some of her pupils are shown here with a donkey cart at the rear of the school buildings. Miss Chinnock's private school was situated in the High Street. Many teachers came to the school from abroad and they were encouraged to instil a love of languages in their pupils. Among the children shown here is Margaret Hooper, whose family came from West Lavington. She stands second from the right. Do you recognise any of these other happy, young faces?

'OUR DAY' IN MARKET LAVINGTON, AT THE TIME OF THE GREAT WAR. 'Our Day' is the photographer's title for this picture-postcard which depicts a sale of work for the Red Cross in 1915. People gave what they could. Here we can see loads of hay, sacks of potatoes, and baskets of vegetables. There are bric-a-brac stalls in the background. The prominent house to the right was once the home of the village doctor. To the left stands the malthouse, of which there were many in the village. The voluntary nurse, pictured in the centre foreground, is Edith Bevan, a local teacher.

SCHOOL DAYS, BEFORE 1913. Here we can see the boys' section at Market Lavington National School. John Duck, the headmaster, can be seen in the midst of the group of boys. We are looking down from the churchyard where the vicar, Revd J.A. Sturton, was able to keep an eye on the children. The girls' playground (only a quarter the size of this one) was at the back of the school. Before 1914, the boys and girls were taught separately after the infant stage. A story survives from 1881 that tells how Mr Duck had the misfortune to catch the mumps from one of his pupils. He obviously made a full recovery, however, because he lived a further thirty-two years. The school closed in 1971.

THE FIRST LAVINGTON GIRL GUIDES' TROOP, EARLY 1920s. The girls, pictured here in Mr Burgess's studio, all came from Market Lavington, although the local detachment was based at West Lavington. Edna Mills and Winnie Mundy stand at the back, second and third from the right. We do not know the name of the guide on the left. Winnie Cooper sits to the right next to Queenie Bullock, and May Spiers is seated on the left.

A RAG-AND-BONE MAN VISITS MARKET LAVINGTON IN THE EARLY TWENTIETH CENTURY. Billy Davis is the dealer pictured here with his donkey cart in Northbrook. We can see that the road leads up towards the Market Place. Many of the houses on the right have been demolished. The photographer would appear to have gone to some lengths to get an interesting picture. The photographic technology of the time was the cause of great fascination to village folk. It is unlikely that a 'stills' photographer in this busy modern age of ours would be able to find enough passers-by with the time or the patience to stand around waiting for a single picture to be taken. A television cameraman, however, would probably have no problem getting volunteers to appear on his digital video recording!

RE-HANGING THE MARKET LAVINGTON CHURCH BELLS IN 1927. Messrs Taylor of Loughborough had the task of restoring the bells of St Mary's Church within a new steel frame to replace the previous wooden structure. Here we can see a bell being lowered from the belfry. Joe Gye stands on the left, with Taylor's representative in the middle. Revd J.A. Sturton and an unidentified man appear on the right side of the picture. Joe Gye was the second generation of his family to be a bell ringer. Today, his grandson is the fourth.

THE WEST LAVINGTON LADIES' FOOTBALL TEAM OF 1920. This six-a-side team took part in a fête during that year. Marjorie Ross (a local school teacher), Lottie Fielding, Mrs Eva Collins, Nancy Barer, May Draper, or Maud Wright, are all believed to be among the ladies in this group.

A CHARABANC OUTING OF THE MID-1920s. A party of day-trippers from West Lavington are seen here in Canal, Salisbury. In the holiday season, throughout the 1920s and 1930s, Harold Whitworth was often to be seen in the Pig Market area of Canal, waiting for the holidaymakers to arrive in their charabancs so that he could take pictures of them (just like the one you see here). Harold was a popular photographer who rode around on a bicycle with a parrot (or a similar kind of bird) perched on his shoulder. There are still people living in Salisbury who remember his birds quite well because one of them used to squawk rather rude, but amusing, utterances about Adolf Hitler. When the day-trippers were on their return journeys, via Salisbury, Harold would have developed the films that he had exposed in the morning and produced postcards of the day-trippers to sell at about 3d each. If the number of surviving Whitworth photographs is anything to go by, then thousands of them were produced. On this particular outing, the conveyance was AM-9698, Commercar charabanc No. 5 from the Lavington & Devizes Motor Services fleet, of which Fred Sayers was the proprietor. The business was taken over by the Bath Tramways Company in the 1930s.

THE DAUNTSEY AGRICULTURAL SCHOOL, WEST LAVINGTON, IN 1913. The accumulated funds of Alderman William Dauntsey's foundation provided the money to build this school, which opened in 1895. During the Second World War, land army girls from all over England trained here for a month in agricultural skills before being sent to work on farms. After the war it was gradually transformed into the respected public school that we know today.

THE ALMSHOUSES AT WEST LAVINGTON, 1914. The houses were originally built under the will of William Dauntsey, who died in 1553. In 1810, they were rebuilt in brick with the central wooden clock tower that can be seen in this picture. 'The crowned maiden' is displayed over the doorway to the right. It is the symbol of the Mercers Company, who were the administrators of these dwellings. In 1975, the ten almshouses were converted into five residences known as Dauntsey Court. The clock tower has gone.

A CHEERFUL PARTY AT THE BELL INN, TILSHEAD, IN THE EARLY 1930s. The Bell Inn, now a private residence, is believed to be the oldest building in the village. The landlord throughout the 1920s and 1930s was Charles Franklin. The butchers' vans pictured here in the forecourt of the pub are both from Heytesbury. Polden's Model T Ford (AM 5054) is nearest to the camera, with Cook's Dodge (MR 85) parked behind it. It seems remarkable that two butchers should have been supported by such a small community as Heytesbury – but at that time it was a flourishing commercial area with its own railway station on the Great Western line.

A SCENE AT ORCHESTON SAINT MARY, AFTER THE GREAT WAR. The buildings on the immediate right are known as flood cottages. They were built after the great flood of 1841, which caused much distress in villages all over Salisbury Plain. Here lived the Smiths, Mr and Mrs Hibberd, and the Misses Oram. Beyond the cottages stands the grocery shop and post office that was for many years run by John Dewey, his wife and three sons. At the very end of the line of buildings can be seen the farm cottage of Thomas, Charles and Jane Allen. Notice the interesting topiary displayed in front of the flood cottages.

TEXT COTTAGE AT ORCHESTON SAINT GEORGE, BEFORE THE GREAT WAR. It is clearly understood why the cottage was so named. Four tiles of Biblical text had been set into the wall around the upstairs window. The triangular tile at the top of the display reads 'Fear God' and the two square ones announce 'Honour the King' and 'Be good unto all men'. The large panel below the window carries the words 'Train up a child in the way he should go and when he is old he will not depart from it'. At around the time of the First World War, a fire took hold in the thatched roof of a neighbouring barn, from which the flames spread to Text Cottage and it was destroyed. The texts have survived and one has been preserved in a nearby garden.

A DOUBLE WEDDING AT ORCHESTON SAINT GEORGE, 15 APRIL 1914. The picture records the wedding of Agnes Hall to Louis Chant, and Clifford Hall to Eva Grist. Sadly, John Hall, the father of Agnes and Clifford and landlord of the Crown Inn, had died just before the wedding. The group photograph was set up on the lawn at the back of the inn. These were the first weddings in the village for which a motor car was used to transport the brides. Two of the bridesmaids pictured in the front row, Vera Chant (later Mrs Bush) and Grace Durley (later Mrs Watson), are still alive and in their nineties.

A RICK FIRE AT ELSTON HILL, 29 AUGUST 1913. In any small rural community, news of an unusual event such as this would spread almost as quickly as the fire itself, and in this particular case, farm labourers and numerous other local people soon arrived with buckets of water and other implements to help fight the flames. A horse-drawn water bowser had also been brought in from a local farm to give an easily accessible, albeit limited, supply of water. A telephone call was made to the Salisbury City Police, who in turn notified the Salisbury Volunteer Fire Brigade. Within minutes, the motor fire tender 'Fawcett' was dispatched with an officer and crew. Although it was running on solid tyres, the 50hp Commercar appliance (AM 2779) could speed along at about 25-30mph. It probably took about thirty minutes to reach the scene of the fire, and it must have been a great relief to the farmer once the professional firefighters had arrived. The 'Fawcett' can be seen parked in the background. It was a very new machine, having only been put into service by the Salisbury Volunteer Fire Brigade a few weeks earlier. The photograph was taken by Albert Marett.

HARVEST FESTIVAL AT SHREWTON BAPTIST CHAPEL, 1916. This photograph was taken at a time when the chapel fairly fizzed with activity as it had a very big influence on the local village population. One of its members was Albert Victor Chant, who joined the Wiltshire Regiment when the First World War started. He was almost immediately taken prisoner in France and put to work on a farm. His health suffered and he died the day before Armistice Day. A plaque was later placed in the chapel in his memory. At the time of writing, the chapel is closed and is awaiting redevelopment. It is thought that the minister seen here is Revd William Samuel Wyle.

THE CATHERINE WHEEL, HIGH STREET, SHREWTON, IN AROUND 1920. George Oliphant, a magistrate and landowner from Elston Hill, kept a pack of bloodhounds at that time. The lady sitting side-saddle on the second horse from the left is believed to be his only child, Jean. Louis Chant can be seen standing in the doorway. The licensee of this popular local hostelry from the time of the First World War and right through the 1920s and 1930s was Reginald Charles Wright. At the time of writing, the pub is boarded up and awaiting redevelopment.

WILLIAM 'BILL' ROSS WITH HIS FAMILY AT SHREWTON. Like Albert Marett, another Shrewton photographer, Bill Ross travelled around the army camps on Salisbury Plain taking pictures of the troops. He also ran a grocery and provisions store in the High Street (a picture of which has been reproduced on page 87). Here we can see the family setting off for a ride on their Clyno motorcycle and sidecar. Their home, Shrewton Lodge, comes into view behind them. Bill's full name was William Alexander Mitchelson Ross. Born in 1883, he passed away in 1957 at the age of seventy-four. He married Rose Wilhelmina Langdon (1885-1968) and by the time of this photograph, they had two children, Harold and Gwen.

MILLIE CHANT AT SHREWTON IN THE EARLY TWENTIETH CENTURY. Millie Chant was the daughter of Henry and Rimmellion Chant, the Shrewton bakers. Their shop, outside of which this picture was taken, was situated in the thoroughfare off the Salisbury Road known today as Chant's Lane. In July 1911, she married Charlie Young who, during their courtship, had been an apprentice carpenter in the village. Later, he worked at Basingstoke and if he could not get home for the weekend, Millie would cycle the long road to Basingstoke and meet him halfway. It can be seen that her bicycle was very well made – it has many accessories fitted, including a saddlebag, saddle cloth, tyre pump, chain guard, rear wheel net, bell, and handlebar grips. The cycle has the appearance of a Humber ladies' model from around 1906.

WILLIAM ROSS'S GENERAL STORE AT SHREWTON IN THE INTER-WAR YEARS.
Bill Ross's shop was well situated in the village. The shop fascia on the left advertises the various facets of his business: 'Radio and Accessories, Leather Goods, Stationery, Photographic Goods and Electrical Fittings'. This is where Bill developed his films, printed his photographs, and published numerous postcards. His daughter Gwen stands in the doorway. Bill can be seen in the centre of the picture in front of a cigarette-dispensing machine, with his youngest son, Ronnie, who often used to ride around the village on this trade bike. The unit on the right was the grocery outlet, at the entrance to which stands his wife, Rose. The man on the right is unknown to us. Bill moved to this shop next to St Mary's Church at the beginning of the First World War. It is now a private house.

*Opposite:* SHREWTON CARNIVAL, 1936. Gwen Cole remembers winning a silver sugar basin for the Ladies' Ankle Competition on this occasion! The carnival parade, led by the village band, usually finished up in this field, called 'the Bury', which is situated behind the Flood Houses. Occasionally, however, it was held at Shrewton Hall Park, the home of Lord and Lady Hinde. Floats came from many of the surrounding villages. The cart in the centre of the picture carries the name Smith, of Imber, and to the right stands the Milk Marketing Board entry, which features a mechanical cow.

THE AVENUE, WINTERBOURNE STOKE, 1911. You are looking up the little hill towards St Peter's Church, which lies at the end. Mr Fry lived in the thatched cottage shown on the left. He worked in Harold Dyer's butcher's shop. The houses that come into view in the distance were part of the Druid's Lodge estate.

CORONATION DAY AT WINTERBOURNE STOKE, 12 MAY 1937. The Coronation of King George VI was celebrated with much enthusiasm all over Great Britain. Here at Winterbourne Stoke, the day commenced with a fancy dress parade which was led by the Shrewton Silver Band. The procession started at the schoolyard and ended on the Manor House lawn, which can be seen in this picture. Among the large number of entrants, the West family figured prominently among the winners, who were judged by Mr and Mrs Parsons, Mrs Wales, and Mrs Lindly. Pillow fights and attempts to climb the greasy pole created much amusement for the children. At 4.15p.m. the youngsters were entertained to tea and each child was presented with a Coronation mug and a new three-penny piece. The adults concluded their day with a dinner, organised by Mr H.G. Alexander, and a smoking party.

# Five

# Amesbury and the
# Avon Valley

THE HIGH STREET, UPAVON, IN THE MID-TWENTIETH CENTURY. The old market square is still evident although markets have not been held there since the early 1800s. The Ingleside Café and general provisions store are to be seen directly ahead, with the road to Pewsey continuing to its right. The Ship Inn lies on the extreme right of the picture. The village of Upavon, situated on the northern fringes of Salisbury Plain, was the home of the Central Flying School, which was active during both world wars. Created in 1912, after the formation of the Royal Flying Corps, it had, among its first students, Major H.M. Trenchard, who later became known as 'The Father of the Royal Air Force'.

HOSPITAL SUNDAY AT NETHERAVON, 1909. The age-old problem of poverty was still evident in South Wiltshire at the time of this photograph. Hospital Sunday was an annual event that was held in many local villages to raise funds for the poor who, as inpatients or outpatients, needed treatment at Salisbury Infirmary. Accompanying the Figheldean Brass Band on this particular occasion were members of the Netheravon Friendly Benefit Society, the local branch of the Ancient Order of Foresters, and the Slate Clubs of Figheldean and Netheravon.

FIGHELDEAN HOUSE, 1905. Almost the entire village was taken over by the War Department in 1898. One of three large houses in the village at that time, Figheldean House, was commandeered for use as officers' quarters. Colonel Edward Agar was in residence when Enos Sheppard, of Figheldean Post Office, published this rather uninteresting picture postcard. Early photographs of the village are very hard to find.

THE RIVER AVON AT MILSTON AT THE TIME OF THE GREAT WAR. Milston lies along the road from Amesbury to Pewsey. This idyllic scene was photographed on a bend of the river just north of Durrington. Joseph Addison, statesman, poet and essayist, was born here in 1672, his father being the rector at that time. Richard May and his son worked the water mill along the Avon in 1920 and they lived in this house. Even at that time, there was no shop in the area, and the children had to travel to Bulford, Durrington or Figheldean to attend school.

A BATHING PARTY AT LARKHILL IN 1913. Open-air bathing on Salisbury Plain, with the wind blowing underneath the corrugated iron barriers, would require a stoical disposition. This pool at Larkhill would appear to have an electric light fitted above it, which would indicate that it was even used at night (or possibly it is a shower head). Army restrictions forbade the use of rivers and other watercourses for recreational purposes unless official permission had been given. Because of the difficulty of providing sufficient hot water in many camps, Southern Command set up a Military Bathing Centre at the Market House (now the public library) in Salisbury. The problem of getting there, of course, proved to be a problem.

A FIELD FORGE AT LARKHILL, 1906. Before the Great War, there were very few permanent buildings in the Larkhill area, and military personnel were accommodated in tents. Apart from Territorial regiments, brigades from Aldershot often arrived on the Plain to take their annual gun practice courses on the ranges. The men marched there and back with an overnight rest break at Popham, near Basingstoke. In this photograph we can see three farriers from 149 Battery, Royal Field Artillery.

A PHOTO OPPORTUNITY AT ROLLESTONE CAMP IN THE 1920s. This was a typical motor transport yard of the time. There had been a radical reduction of personnel and materials by 1921 and there was very little money available to invest in new military equipment. Among the vehicles pictured here in the background are several re-conditioned machines from the First World War. There are two FWD balloon winches (made by the Four Wheel Drive Auto Company of Wisconsin, USA), a Leyland truck, a Crossley tender, a Morris Commercial mobile office, a Buick ambulance and a Trojan utility. The names of the airmen are recorded as follows: (standing) Lac, Cooper, Partridge, Jones, Pope, Banish, and Herber; (seated) Angus, Foley, Flt Officer Hall, Sqn Leader C.F. Gordon, Mr Ewason, and Cpl Rose.

EMPIRE AIR DAY AT THE RAF BALLOON SCHOOL, LARKHILL, 1935. The event took place at Rollestone on 25 May. A group of schoolchildren were being shown one of the huge balloons that were kept in the hangars because of rough weather.

A FRUIT AND VEG HAWKER AT THE STONEHENGE INN, DURRINGTON, IN 1916. On the right we can see Frank Henry Witt, of 22 Greencroft Street, Salisbury, who, at the time of the First World War, travelled around the southern areas of Salisbury Plain selling fruit, vegetables, and wet fish. At that time he was offering mackerel at twelve shillings a pound, kippers at six shillings, and bloaters at fourteen shillings. Sometimes, Frank would take his son Donald out on the rounds, as he did on this particular day. The lad can be seen here in the driving position at the front of the wagon. When travelling out to Durrington, they would go via the Woodford Valley, making house calls on the way. The photograph was taken by Marcus Bennett, of the Durrington and Bulford Camp Studios, who had formerly worked for Tom Fuller in Amesbury.

THE STONES AND ALL SAINTS CHURCH, DURRINGTON, 1912. To the right we can see the medieval-cross stones which marked a pre-Christian site. They had broken down a long time ago but after the First World War they were surmounted by a new cross to become the village war memorial. This was the meeting place for many parish events and also the spot from which Frank Toomer, in his role as Agent for the Winchester College properties, had the unenviable task of selling off the furniture of tenants who could not pay their rent.

A GATHERING AT THE DURRINGTON STONES IN 1899. During this year, a photographer of the Climax Photographic Company of 20 Cheapside, London, toured around the villages and hamlets of South Wiltshire taking pictures of the local people, their homes, their places of work, the public buildings, and general views of the environment. It was no doubt a very successful enterprise, as very few people would have owned a camera at that time. The prints that they were sold would have probably been the first ones that many of the families would have seen of themselves, their homes or their local schools. A number of the images taken at Durrington have survived, including this one of a group of young men. Lewis Toomer stands at the back, on the left, with Walter Fudge to the right. Between them, in a lower position, can be seen Norman Graham, and on the same level also stands Arthur Weeks. In the front row, from left to right, we can see Charles Gardiner, Edwin Toomer, Master Hunt, Fred Spreadbury, Fred Fudge, Sid Hunt, and Reggie Moore. The very young boy seated on the lower level is Charles Smith. This was a regular Sunday meeting place.

HARRY HORSELL OUTSIDE HIS DURRINGTON HOME. Harry was a businessman who lived in this cottage in College Lane with his daughters Mary and Elizabeth. In his spare time, he would go round the corner to the Church Room (previously the school) to read the *Times* newspaper to a number of agricultural labourers who were unable to read for themselves. After his death, his home was renamed Horsell House in his memory.

DURRINGTON SCHOOL, 1925. These children are from Class 1, Standards 2 and 3. Only three of the children are thought to be still alive as the twentieth century draws to an end. Among those to be seen in the back row are, Harold Smith, Liberty Green, Edna Toomer, and Muriel Hall. The second row includes Ronnie Freeman, Ruby Lewis, and Sophie Heaver, while the third row includes a child named Egginton, Freda Baker, the two Murdoch sisters, Connie Christie, and a boy named Cook. Reggie Case can be seen in the front row, as well as Mabel Read, Lily Root, Topsy Hargreaves, Margaret Solman, another child from the Root family, and Joan Cosgrove. In the group, somewhere, are Linda Sturgess, Ida Clark, and a child named Rogers. Perhaps you can recognise them?

'HARRY' FROOM IN HIS DURRINGTON WORKSHOP. A fitter and welder by trade, Harry opened a garage in Durrington that sold petrol and cars; he was a resourceful individual who could turn his hand to almost anything. He was very good with electricity and later became one of the directors and chief engineer of the Durrington Electric Light Company. When he died suddenly in 1944, at the age of fifty-two, he left a widow, their son Jack, and three daughters. A picture of Harry as a young man serving in the Army Service Corps at Bulford has been reproduced on page 118.

A GENERAL VIEW OF AMESBURY IN THE 1930s. We are looking from the Lynchets down on to the Salisbury Road as it makes its way northwards into the town. The former workhouse, shown on the immediate left, was completed in 1837 to serve a union of twenty-three neighbouring parishes. It had room for 150 inmates and included dormitories, sick wards, wash houses, a school and a chapel. Avonstoke Close now stands on the site.

DIANA HOUSE AND COUNTESS BRIDGE, AMESBURY, IN THE EARLY 1900s. The building on the left carries the inscription 'Diana her House 1600'. Its original purpose is uncertain but a boathouse, hunting lodge or even the residence of an official of the adjoining Amesbury Abbey Estate have all been suggested. Sadly, this quiet rural setting has been eroded by the intrusions of modern traffic. The A303 and Countess Roundabout now lie on the other side of the bridge. The picture postcard comes from a series produced by WH Smith.

Cold Harbour. Amesbury.

Tucker
Amesbury.

SMITHFIELD STREET AND COLDHARBOUR, AMESBURY, BEFORE 1914. The Greyhound Inn, run at that time by John Harnes, can be seen on the right. To the left stands George Bailey's dairy cart, which carried a seventeen-gallon milk churn. Coldharbour was originally a broad droveway, sometimes 150 feet in width, along which sheep and cattle were herded from the east pasture to the livestock market near this point.

THE QUEENSBERRY AND BELL HOTELS, AMESBURY, AFTER THE FIRST WORLD WAR. These buildings face Salisbury Street, which was originally twice the width that it is today, with large mature trees down the centre. Nearest to the camera is the Queensberry House Hotel, which is now a solicitor's office. At the time of this photograph, Mr Frank Tucker was the proprietor. He placed an advertisement in *The Graphic Guide to Amesbury* (published *c.* 1910) which describes the hotel as 'A Home from Home, with well appointed bedrooms, hot and cold baths, private sitting rooms, all recently enlarged'. Next to Queensberry House stands Mrs Bessie Treasure's steam bakery and grocery stores. Then coming into view is the Bell Hotel which was built in 1908. There were two managers in the years immediately following the First World War: William Malone and Charles Mannell.

MARY JANE MORTIMER, AN AMESBURY LAUNDRESS. Mary Jane lived with her husband Harry, a civil engineer, in a large house in Salisbury Street. At the beginning of the twentieth century, with Salisbury Plain being used increasingly for military purposes, they started a steam laundry. The business flourished as a growing number of trips were made around the Plain to collect and deliver laundry. The 'rounds' would take in large houses like Amesbury Abbey and Wilsford Manor House, plus local pubs and clubs and several army camps. Many of the young people who worked in the laundry came from St Mary's Home (near St Martin's church) in Salisbury, which accommodated children from difficult backgrounds. Harry died in 1916, at which time there was a shortage of male labour to repair machinery. These factors seriously hindered the business and it was closed in the following year. Mary Jane died in 1930. A supermarket stands on the site of her laundry today.

A NINETEENTH-CENTURY AMESBURY VICARAGE. Built on the site of the eighteenth-century Chopping Knife Inn, the building was owned by the well-known local Pinckney family. It was sold to the Reverend Meyrick, who opened a highly respected school to the left of the picture (now a private residence). The building was later to become a temperance hotel, then the Avon Hotel. It is now known as the Antrobus Arms Hotel.

SALISBURY STREET, AMESBURY, AT THE TIME OF THE SECOND WORLD WAR. A Leyland TS8 coach from the Wilts and Dorset fleet (BWV 672) can be seen approaching, in the middle of the road, en route to Salisbury via Amesbury. It has a typical wartime appearance with white-painted edges to the wings and masked headlights. Despite the fact that Great Britain was at war, there was still much commercial activity going on in Salisbury Street. Among the businesses to be found here were Hugh Bascomb-Harrison, chemist; Mrs A.W. Dyke's refreshment rooms; Jackson, Hodding & Company, solicitors; John Molsher, hairdresser; A.T. Noyce, bakers; Philip Pethen, newsagent, (pictured on the left); Herbert J. Ridout, general stores; The Misses Tucker's Queensberry House, private hotel; Albert Tucker, grocer; Mrs E. Walker's drapery; Thomas Wright, car hire; Richard Yapp, baker and grocer; Percy Underwood, Bell Hotel; and Albert Zebedee, family butcher. Chipperfield's Circus had their winter quarters in a yard close to where the lady stands on the right.

AN AVELING & PORTER STEAM ROAD-ROLLER NEAR AMESBURY. A Wiltshire County Council road maintenance gang are seen at work in the early 1900s. Although the Invicta steamroller was available for the heavy work, a pair of horse-drawn trucks was also used to carry tools and road re-surfacing materials.

THE LAST TRAIN OUT OF AMESBURY, 1963. The first train arrived at Amesbury Station on the London & South Western Railway on 2 June 1902. From rather quiet beginnings, the station developed into a frantic military communications centre, its four platforms often packed with army personnel and equipment. When peacetime conditions returned after 1945, Amesbury Railway Station gradually lost out to the road transport industry. Although passenger traffic ceased in 1952, goods were carried until 1965. Here we can see *The Rambling Rose*, a Class M7 locomotive, No. 30108, making its last sad journey on 23 March, 1963. The station stood to the south of the London Road where, today, the Amesbury Transport Company and other light industries are to be found.

A DISTANT VIEW OF STONEHENGE, BEFORE 1912. This classic photograph was taken from the hill overlooking the junction of the Exeter (now the busy A303) and Devizes roads. The image is reproduced from a picture postcard that carries a half-penny stamp and a Bustard Camp postmark dated 10 August 1912. Perhaps the soldiers in the horse-drawn runabout were stationed at Bustard? The buildings that come into view on the horizon, to the left, may well have been part of the Stonehenge airfield.

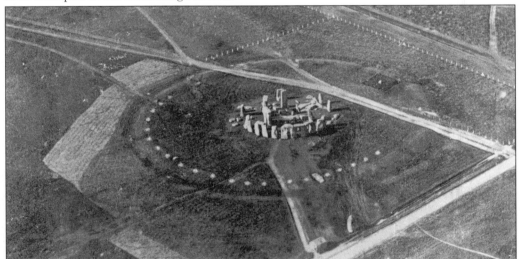

STONEHENGE FROM THE AIR IN THE EARLY 1920s. At the beginning of the twentieth century, these famous stones were part of the Amesbury Abbey Estate, owned by the Antrobus family. In 1915, however, Knight, Frank & Rutley were instructed to sell the land. Lot 15 was described as 'Stonehenge – 30 acres of grazing'. Because of various restrictions, however, little interest was shown in the pre-historic site but Cecil Chubb, then director of the Fisherton House Lunatic Asylum in Salisbury, purchased it for just £6,600. Three years later he presented Stonehenge to the nation. A Durrington farmer named Frank Toomer was also present at the sale. He had hoped to acquire the land for grazing sheep and was later heard to exclaim, wryly, that if he had bought the plot he would probably have taken the stones down for building materials!

A SCENE AT WEST AMESBURY, AFTER THE GREAT WAR. What could be more typical of rural tranquillity than this Woodford Valley view in the early twentieth century? Separated from the town by the River Avon, the village consists mainly of cob, thatch and brick cottages that were formerly dwellings of farm tenants and have now been transformed into attractive private homes. West Amesbury House, a sixteenth and seventeenth century chequer stone and flint construction, contains traces of a medieval building that is believed to have been associated with Amesbury Abbey. There was also a strong nonconformist tradition in the village. In 1669, thirty people crammed into the small cottage of Thomas Long, an Anabaptist, for their Sunday services!

LAKE HOUSE, IN THE WOODFORD VALLEY, BEFORE 1910. Built in the seventeenth century, with its beautiful wooded grounds near the Avon, this mansion is in the ancient parish of Wilsford. From 1897, it was owned by Joseph Lovibond, who was Lord of the Manor and a wealthy industrialist of his time. The house was destroyed by fire on Good Friday 1912, but fortunately the family were then living in a smaller house on the estate. The house was rebuilt and today it is the home of the popular musician 'Sting' and his family.

HEALE HOUSE, MIDDLE WOODFORD, BEFORE 1913. Built in 1585, Heale House brought a moment of historic significance to the Woodford Valley when Charles II was concealed here, the home of Katherine Hyde, while on the run after the Battle of Worcester. Its eight acres of beautiful gardens are largely unchanged since that time. Among the displays of flowers and speciality roses that are admired throughout the summer season is an authentic Japanese Tea House and Nikko bridge.

ALL SAINTS CHURCH, MIDDLE WOODFORD, EARLY TWENTIETH CENTURY. Among the grander plaques to be found on the walls of this church is a more humble one to a domestic servant who gave sixty years of devoted service to her employer. All Saints Church is of Norman origin but it was largely rebuilt in 1845. The Reverend Samuel Fraser was the vicar around this time. The picture is reproduced from one of a series of postcards published by 'Charlie' May of Gomeldon Hill, near Porton. From around 1900 until the 1930s, he was a regular visitor to the villages of the Woodford Valley.

A SPECIAL DELIVERY TO THE WOODFORD VALLEY. Percy Harold Elliott is pictured here delivering groceries to clients in the Woodford Valley. For a number of years, he helped his father run a wholesale grocery supply business from their base at 6 Avon View, off Castle Street, Salisbury. The family also operated the pleasure boats that were kept at the Avon Boathouse at the back of Castle Street. Percy's means of transport on this particular day was a 1913 James 3.5hp motorcycle and sidecar. He may look familiar to those of you who have enjoyed browsing through the pages of some of the other Wiltshire books that Peter Daniels and Rex Sawyer have produced. Harold delighted in a few hours of fame when, in January 1915, he put some of his boats to work ferrying people up and down Fisherton Street, which was under fourteen inches of water following a prolonged spell of heavy rain. It was the worst flood that the city had experienced for many years. Photographers came here from all over the south of England to take pictures of the unusual scenes. Very many photographs were published, and quite a number of the surviving examples show Harold in one or other of his boats.

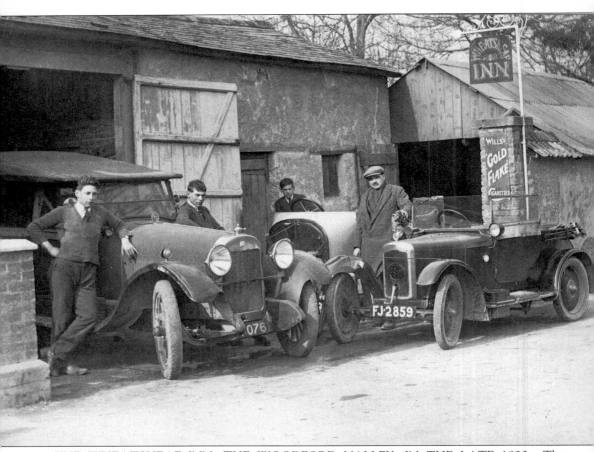

THE WHEATSHEAF INN, THE WOODFORD VALLEY, IN THE LATE 1920s. The western valley road passes through the three Woodford villages. This eighteenth-century inn, which lies in Lower Woodford, was originally a farm. At the beginning of the twentieth century it was run by the Deare family and their descendants. At one time, ten members of the family were living and working in the inn, which is still a popular hostelry today. The car on the left is a Buick (made in Detroit, USA) and the little model on the right is an 8hp Rover, which carries an Exeter registration plate (FJ 2859). Pictured behind them is a third vehicle which has its engine cover removed for repair or servicing perhaps.

*Opposite:* ST ANDREW'S CHURCH, DURNFORD, EARLY IN THE TWENTIETH CENTURY. Hidden in the Woodford Valley is this fine example of a Norman church, which is surprisingly large for such a small village. It still retains traces of medieval wall paintings and it has a fine Norman font, which can be seen in the centre of this picture. Revd Leicester Selby was the rector at this time.

THE MANOR HOUSE LOWER WOODFORD, IN THE LATE-NINETEENTH CENTURY.
This gracious residence, now known as the Manor House, was, in earlier times, the home of the
Chief Freeholder of the parish. It lies north of the Wheatsheaf Inn, but unlike the other houses
there, it stands back from the road in its own grounds. This is almost certainly the house built
by George Davis when he was Chief Freeholder immediately after the Restoration, though the
semi-basement would appear to be older than that. Built of mellow-brick with stone quoins, the
Manor House is now the home of the Rasch family.

THATCHED COTTAGES IN THE WOODFORD VALLEY IN THE 1930s. This charming view is reproduced on a picture postcard entitled 'Thatched cottages at Great Durnford'. It is believed, however, that the houses are actually situated across the River Avon at Wilsford-Cum-Lake. They are typical of the fashionable thatched residences found up and down the Woodford Valley which were originally homes of poor agricultural labourers.

# Six

# Around
# the Bourne Valley

THE BLUE LION AND RAILWAY HOTEL, COLLINGBOURNE DUCIS, AFTER THE GREAT WAR. This picture, from the early 1920s, was taken at a time when the management of the hotel was changing. Henry Wright took on the license, which had previously been held by Mrs Emily Maria Cass, a widow. On the opposite side of the road can be seen the Model T Ford tourer (HR 683) in which the photographer Joseph James ('JJ') Hunt travelled around Wiltshire taking pictures. He had a very successful practice with studios in Ludgershall, Marlborough and Calne. His wife is presumably the lady sitting in the car.

'BRUCE', A MUCH-LOVED REGIMENTAL MASCOT, 1909. The dog, seen here with his young escort, was the cherished pet of the 4th Wiltshire Regiment. Most companies had their own mascot, some of which were quite exotic. The Royal Field Artillery at Larkhill, for example, had a monkey!

HIGH STREET AND CASTLE STREET, LUDGERSHALL, 1908. William Cobbett, in 1826, described Ludgershall as 'one of the most mean and beggarly places that man ever set his eyes on'. In fact it has a long and colourful history. The ruins of the castle still remind us of its influence on the area since the eleventh century. It was once thought to be the premier castle in Britain. This ancient borough was revitalised in 1902 with the construction of the railway. With increasing military activities on Salisbury Plain, Ludgershall played an important role in both world wars as a military communications centre.

*Opposite:* THE 4TH WILTS ARRIVING AT LUDGERSHALL STATION IN 1909. Men from the 4th Wiltshire Regiment are seen here detraining at Ludgershall before marching off to their summer training camp. The troops had arrived in third-class carriages on this L & SWR train. The Ludgershall to Tidworth line had opened in 1901. It was the first railway to be built on the Plain with the primary objective of servicing the rapidly growing military camps. Trains carrying both men and equipment completely transformed the quiet village into one of the busiest communications centres in the area. George Humphries was the stationmaster at the time of this picture.

113

ST JAMES' CHURCH, LUDGERSHALL. The church was still being illuminated by gas lights when this picture was taken, and it had been lavishly decorated for a special occasion – a harvest festival, perhaps? St James' has a long and historic past. A stone near the entrance is of Saxon origin and the foundations and font, which can be seen on the left of the picture, are Norman. The tomb of Sir Richard and Lady Jane Brydges, ancestors of the late Princess Diana, are lodged here.

THE DRUMS OF THE 1ST WILTS 'SPRING CLEANING' IN 1914. These soldiers from the 1st Wiltshire Corps of Drums are taking a welcome break from barrack room 'bulling' at Tidworth. Surprisingly, they seem to be enjoying the experience! The soldier standing on the extreme left is known to us simply as 'GH'. He wrote the following note to a girlfriend, Miss Brown, of Worcester Villa, 92 Parkwood Road, Bournemouth, in February 1914: 'Dear Mabel, What do you think of a rough mob like this just as we finished white-washing our room out, me with the mop?'

THE POST OFFICE AT NORTH TIDWORTH BEFORE THE FIRST WORLD WAR. The postbox that is fitted in the window, to the left of the shop doorway, is still embossed with Queen Victoria's initials 'VR'. The postmaster at that time was Edward Eyles. He was a very busy man who, in addition to running the post office, was the village carrier, travelling to Salisbury on Tuesdays and to Andover on Wednesdays and Fridays. He also managed the grocery and draper's shops in the village. In more recent times this post office has served as a newsagents and a fancy goods shop.

ST MARY'S CHURCH, TIDWORTH, IN 1905. When the army acquired the Tedworth Estate in 1897, there were two churches there: the ancient church of Holy Trinity in North Tidworth, and this church of St Mary's in South Tidworth which was built in 1879. Situated near Tedworth House, it continued to serve the community until 1972, when it was declared redundant. The first church specifically designed for the army was the garrison church of St Andrew and St Mark, which opened in 1909.

A MEMENTO OF THE IAN HAMILTON WESLEYAN SOLDIERS' HOME, TIDWORTH. After the completion of the army barracks at Tidworth in 1905, it became apparent that something needed to be done for the welfare of the troops when they were off duty. This was the first of three such institutes created for that purpose. The building, constructed by C. Grace & Sons, was named after the Commander-in-Chief, Lieutenant General Sir Ian Hamilton, and opened on 4 July 1908. The building can still be seen near the main entrance to the garrison. We believe that the woman shown here is Sister Dora Stephenson but we have not been able to identify the gentleman. Do you know who he is?

TIDWORTH RAILWAY STATION, BEFORE 1920. After much delay due to army resistance, this was the first line to be built on Salisbury Plain. Opened in July 1902, it was linked to the main Midland and South Western Junction Railway at Ludgershall, and it incorporated the Tidworth Military Railway. Both systems were built by Henry Lovatt Limited. Until the station's closure in 1958, two locomotives known affectionately as 'Molly' and 'Betty' were often to be seen on the rails carrying straw and feed for the army horses as well as other essential provisions.

A TIDWORTH MILITARY OUTING, AFTER THE FIRST WORLD WAR. Are these sergeants of the Royal Engineers seated in the charabanc anticipating an enjoyable break from duties? Or are they preparing to attend a training seminar? The white cap denotes an officer in summer attire so perhaps the expedition had a more serious purpose. The four-horse charabanc (there is another pair of horses out of view to the right) is a very sturdy machine, which has the appearance of carriages known to have been built by Vincent coach-builders of Reading. The canvas cover strapped to the roof bars can be quickly rolled out if it starts to rain. Access to the rows of benches is made from a pair of steps at the back of the vehicle.

A BULFORD ARMY SERVICE CORPS UNIT AT THE TIME OF THE FIRST WORLD WAR. The platform lorry was supplied by the Albion Motor Car Company Limited, of Scotstoun, Glasgow, for evaluation purposes by the ASC at Bulford. The firm was very successful and it was awarded many contracts to produce soft-skinned and armoured vehicles for use by military units all around the world. The first Albions were made a hundred years ago in 1899. Seated second from the right on this particular machine is Corporal Henry Lionel Corry Froom, known to his friends as Harry. After the war he chose to stay in the area and he built his own home in Durrington. Jack, his son, still lives in the house today. A picture of Harry in later life has been reproduced on page 97.

HAMPSHIRE MEN ON MANOEUVRES AT BULFORD IN 1912. The two-week exercise commenced on 7 September and involved the officers and men of the 9th Hampshire (Cycle) Regiment. Having arrived at the L&SWR station in Salisbury by train (see page 14) the next leg of the unit's journey was to be by road to Sling Plantation, Bulford. The cyclists rode their bicycles while the officers were afforded the luxury of a ride in a fleet of motor cars. The regimental equipment was also carried by road. The heavy items were loaded onto the back of a steam lorry that had been hired from Charles Salter of Winchester. The lighter goods were transported in a Scout motor van that had been leased from Hardy & Sons, mineral water manufacturers, of Brown Street, Salisbury. The locally operated van (AM-1652) had been assembled at the Scout Motor Company works at Bemerton in 1910. In the picture we can see some of the officers' kit being loaded onto the back of the Scout lorry prior to the battalion's move to another location. From Sling Plantation they journeyed to many other places including Shipton Bellinger, Highclere, Basingstoke, Windsor, Slough, St Albans, and Newport Pagnell.

*Opposite*: CAPTAIN ALFRED JAMES 'AJ' ATKINS AND A FRIEND AT BULFORD. This photograph was taken outside the RASC Mess, at Bulford Camp, where 'AJ' was stationed for a time. His dark green, 9.2hp, GMK motorcar (HR 4657) was registered in Wiltshire on the 31 May 1921, some considerable time after it had been manufactured. The first GWK (Grice, Wood & Keillor) cars were made in 1911, firstly in Datchet and later in Maidenhead. This one had two cylinders and a friction-drive gearbox.

WATER STREET, BULFORD, IN THE EARLY 1900s. The Nine Mile River joins the Avon close to this spot near the Bulford Road. A local tradesman would appear to be making a delivery to the cottages. He may have found it difficult to reverse his wagon, as the road narrows to a footpath beyond the white posts. Sadly, the river flow has been depleted in recent years due to the extraction of water for military purposes.

THE ROSE AND CROWN, HIGH STREET, BULFORD, 1916. Before 1900, there were three pubs in Bulford: The Lamb, The Maidenhead, and The Rose and Crown. The latter was constructed in 1844 and rebuilt in 1896. Alfred Leaker was the licensee from 1916 to the early 1920s. He is depicted here standing in front of the pub with his wife. The rest of his staff can just be seen beneath the veranda. Known as 'The Soldiers' Pub', it remains a popular hostelry to this day.

CHURCH LANE, CHOLDERTON, 1918. This view of St Nicholas Church has changed little over the years except that a large portion of the unusual bell tower has been removed. The school, out of sight on the right at the top of the lane, is now a private house. Behind the church is a very unusual house-shaped tomb dedicated to Henry Charles Stephens, the inventor of the famous blue-black writing fluid.

NEWTON TONY SCHOOL, 1910. The rather mature-looking boy on the right, who would appear to be fiddling with his tie, is Harold Armstead, who was born in 1900. His family had been running the village carrier service since the late 1800s, and by 1920, Harold was managing the business himself. Later on, the family ran a bus service from the village into Salisbury using a Leyland Comet coach. When this picture of the pupils was taken, Miss Mabel Tabor was the schoolmistress.

THE VILLAGE HALL, NEWTON TONY, IN THE 1920s. The building was erected in 1920 by Sir Harry Malet, Lord of the Manor, a distinguished soldier and master of the Tedworth Hunt. He was living, at that time, at Wilbury House. He allowed the village to use this building, with its three and a half acres of land, for a recreation ground. The stationmaster, James Norwood, can be seen standing on the right with a small child.

AIL SAINTS CHURCH, IDMISTON, 1905. The vicar at this time was the Reverend George Mallows Youngman, who lived at Porton. The church has features from every period from Norman times onwards, including fifteenth-century carved stone corbels supporting the ends of the roof timbers. They are believed to depict local villagers of the time. Since 1978, the church has been redundant and the congregation has joined that of St Nicholas's Church, Porton.

HIGH STREET, IDMISTON, BEFORE 1918. These cottages lie between Hair Pin Bend and the church. The spire comes into view in the distance. The cottages can still be seen today. On the back of the original picture someone has written the following note: 'This is the road that leads up to the camp grounds at which my husband was stationed in August, 1918. In remembrance of my holiday at Idmiston, 5th-10th August, 1918'.

HALL & SELWAY'S SHOP AT PORTON, 1930s. From early in the twentieth century until the time of the Second World War, George Selway was a jack-of-all-trades. Among other things, he was the village carrier, a part-time stationmaster, a newsagent, and stationer. It would seem that on at least one occasion, he took part in a promotion for *Hobbies* magazine which was published every other week at 2d a copy. There are *Hobbies* posters, banners and signs displayed all over the front and side of this galvanised iron shop.

AN EDWARDIAN VIEW OF PORTON. In the background of this photograph we can see the grocery shop that Thomas Noyce had been running since before 1899. He was also a beer retailer, jobmaster, and carriage proprietor. By 1911, the business had been sold to Ernest Kail, whose family lived over the shop. They continued to provide a good service to the community for many years. The house nearest to the camera was the home of the local baker, Harold Bailey. It was demolished a long time ago. Of the two individuals pictured in the foreground, the boy would seem to be better equipped to ride a bicycle than the woman – the long skirt must have hindered her progress somewhat.

WINTERBOURNE GUNNER POST AND TELEGRAPH OFFICE, BEFORE 1910. The sub-postmistress at the time was Mrs Emma Smith, who was also the grocer. Throughout much of the ensuing century, however, the post office was associated with Mrs Frances Pocock. She ran the business with her son Edwin, who was always known as Pat because he was born on St Patrick's Day. The post office was closed around forty years ago. Further down the road lie farm cottages and the home of Dr G. Stone, a founder member of the Bourne Valley Historical Society.

GATERS LANE FORD, WINTERBOURNE DAUNTSEY. Although this picture was taken at the dawn of the twentieth century, the scene is not so very different today. In earlier times, the road was known as Kelly's Lane after the family who kept the village store situated on the corner. Just out of the picture to the right stood the home of the miller, Joe Smith, who worked for Bernard White, a local farmer. The original photograph was taken by Charlie May.

HARVEST TEA AT WINTERBOURNE EARLS, 1910. These events traditionally took place on the tennis court at the Rectory. After the tea, entertainment would be provided and in the evening, a thanksgiving service would be held at St Michael's Church, conducted by the vicar, the Reverend Frank Elcho Skyrme. His wife always decorated the church with flowers for these occasions. The church can just be seen through the trees in the background.

WINTERBOURNE DAUNTSEY IN THE 1920s. Straight ahead lie Box Cottages, three homes which are now blended into one and known as Peacock Cottage because of the appropriate topiary in the front garden. Gaters Lane turns off to the left, and the Winterbourne Gunner road is to the right. The thatched building on the left side of the road was the village grocery shop. This was run by Ada Porter and her husband, 'Dot,' who worked on the railway. On the opposite side of the road stands the Club House, an institute that the young men of the village used for recreational activities.

AN OUTING FROM THE WINTERBOURNES TO PORTSMOUTH DOCKS IN 1924. The party left at 8a.m. and did not arrive until nearly midday! In those days, too, it was a requirement that all coaches should leave the seaside resorts by 6.30p.m. Everyone wore their Sunday-best clothes, including the children, and they took a picnic lunch. This particular day out had been organised by Mr Calloway, who is shown on the extreme left of the picture. His son, John, stands in the centre, and his daughter is to the right, holding a basket. Fred Smith stands next to Mr Calloway, and his mother is the sixth adult from the left. Also pictured here among the day trippers are Mary Calloway, Mrs Mouland, and Mrs Rowden and her son, George Bowen.

THE HAMLET OF HURDCOTT BEFORE THE GREAT WAR. During the early twentieth century, Mrs Emma Dimmer (née Elliott) lived in the left-hand cottage of the two shown to the right. The Bedford family lived in the other. Frank Dimmer was a carter and Mr Bedford was a general agricultural labourer. They both worked at George Bright's farm. In the centre of the picture stands Inglenook, to the left of which can be seen the brick and flint end of Three Poplars, taking its name from the trees behind. Riverside, the cottage on the left has survived but it is no longer thatched.

# Acknowledgements

Having already compiled two books of archive photographs depicting the people and places of Salisbury Plain, Rex and I thought that we would experience some difficulty in finding enough material to complete a new album illustrating the life and times of the inhabitants and environs of South Wiltshire. Our initial concerns soon melted away when it became clear that the generous, willing and helpful nature of the people of this region were creating a rather different kind of dilemma for us: the problem of what items to use and which ones to leave out. We are both very grateful for all the help and encouragement received and we regret that a few individuals may be disappointed that their contributions have not been included. It is our intention, however, to produce a follow up, 'a second selection', which will feature some of the images and information omitted this time. We hope to include the Ebble Valley, Downton, Harnham, Laverstock, Salisbury, Wilton and neighbourhood, and more of the exceptional photographs taken by the late Austin Underwood.

Our thanks are due to so many organisations and individuals that have helped to produce what we believe to be an excellent photographic record of life in South Wiltshire during a period of about a hundred years (1860s-1960s). We are particularly grateful for the assistance of Peter Goulding, whose knowledge of Wiltshire railways is to be admired. The members of staff at the Reference and Local Studies Department of Salisbury Library have, as ever, assisted our enquiries at every turn and they thoroughly deserve our gratitude.

The following individuals have all contributed greatly to the project: Donald Andrews (The Langfords); Mary Arnold (Broad Chalke); Maureen Atkinson (Bourne Valley); Frank Bailey (Porton and the Winterbournes); Toby Baker (Tisbury); A.C.J. Bishop (Tisbury); Len Campbell (Netheravon); Rodney Carpenter; Anthony Claydon (East Knoyle); Gwen Cole (Shrewton); Maurice and Paul Cole (Codford); Bunny Corner (Berwick St James); Rosina Corp (Amesbury); Michael Daniels (Imber); Francis Dineley (Berwick St John); Dinton WI Scrapbook, 1956; Stan Everett (Salisbury railways); Jack Froom (The Froom family); Richard and Pat Eckersley (Porton and the Winterbournes); Colin Everall (Wilton); Barbara Fergusson (Ebbesbourne Wake); Ann Ferreira (Broad Chalke); Richard Fraser (Salisbury railways); Robert and Sally Fry (Broad Chalke); Elizabeth Gallup (Bishopstone); Peter Goodhugh (Amesbury); Christine Gulliver (Bowerchalke); Clarence Hardiman (Bowerchalke); Alwyn Hardy (Warminster); George and Pat Heath (Urchfont); Geoffrey Hitchings (Broad Chalke); Mrs Holloway (Wilton); Betty Hooper (Imber); Hilda Hull (Semley); Revd Anthony Johnson (Semley); John Judd (Coombe Bissett); Peggy Gye (Market Lavington); Tim Harding (vintage and veteran cars); Joyce Kelly (Bourne Valley); Nigel Lampard (South Newton); Taffy Leach (*Rambling Rose*); Mrs V. Leather (9th Battalion Hampshire (Cycle) Regiment); Gp Capt. M.J.W. Lee; David Low (Semley); Tony Lyons (Newton Tony); Edith MacPherson (South Newton); Mere Museum; Sandra Mislin (Urchfont); Nancy Morland (Wilton); Kathleen Mould (Tisbury); Gordon Norris (Codford); Norman Parker (RAF balloons); Rex Reynolds (West Amesbury); Edna Richardson (Durrington); Keith Shaw (GWK cars); Judy Sheppard (Bowerchalke); Bubbles Spetch (South Wiltshire churches); Michael Tighe (Mere); Harold Trowbridge (Trowbridge family); Dreda, Lady Tryon (Woodford Valley); Mary Underwood (Amesbury); Mr Underwood (Kilmington); Beryl Wainwright (Elliott family); Gordon Warren (Donhead St Mary); Pauline White (Warminster); Harry Withers (Shrewton); Donald Witt (Witt family); *The Woodford Parish History*, by Margaret Briggs; Romy Wyeth (Codford).

Peter R. Daniels
Netherhampton
July 1999